THE WORLD OF CACTI

THE WORLD OF
CACTI

HOW TO SELECT FROM AND CARE FOR OVER 1000 SPECIES

DANNY SCHUSTER

Photography by J. Koster and K. Winiarski

Facts On File

New York • Oxford • Sydney

Dedicated to Danielle, Caroline, Nicholas, Olivia and Hannah

The World of Cacti

Copyright © 1990 by Danny Schuster

Facts On File, Inc. Facts On File Limited
460 Park Avenue South Collins Street
New York NY 10016 Oxford OX4 1XJ
USA United Kingdom

Library of Congress Cataloguing-in-Publication Data

Schuster, Danny.
  The world of cacti / Danny Schuster.
  240p. 19×26 cm.
  Includes bibliographical references.
  ISBN 0-8160-2506-1 (alk. paper)
  1. Cactus. 2. Cactus — Pictorial works. I. Title.
SB438.S342 1990
635.9'3347 — dc20

A British CIP catalogue record for this book is available from the British
Library.

Facts On File books are available at special discounts when purchased
in bulk quantities for businesses, associations, institutions or sales
promotions. Please call our Special Sales Department in New York at
(212) 683 2244 (dial (800) 322 8755 except in NY, AK or HI) or in Oxford
at (865) 72 8399.

Designed and produced by Pierson & Co
PO Box 87 Mosman NSW 2088
Sydney Australia
Printed in Singapore by Singapore National Printers
10 9 8 7 6 5 4 3 2 1

CONTENTS

FOREWORD

By Clara M. Maurer

In *What Cactus is That?* Danny Schuster reviews and greatly expands his previous work, *Introduction to Cacti*, from the origins of cacti to the beautiful photographs and detailed descriptions of the Cactaceae. There are over 400 colour photographs in sharp detail of both body and bloom of plants in the Cactaceae family, with easy-to-read descriptions, habitat information, and other data helpful to the grower. Cactus collectors, both beginner and advanced, many times have difficulty identifying plants purchased from nurseries that grow merely for the commercial market, and this book is a tremendous aid for this purpose.

The chapter on growing cacti from seed gives step by step instructions, with illustrations, and will make the reader eager to acquire seed and attempt this fascinating, although sometimes frustrating, phase of the cactus hobby. Other methods of propagation, such as by offsets or by grafting, are also described very thoroughly. Instructions for several methods of grafting are given, again with illustrations, and, important in my opinion, the reasons for grafting.

Soil, light, temperature requirements, planting in various types of containers, as well as in outdoor beds, are discussed thoroughly but concisely. Several pages are devoted to causes of deformations of plants with suggestions for possible cures, and to some of the most common insect pests that attack cactus.

What Cactus is That? is not only an excellent reference book, the chapters on culture can also be read over and over, and each time something new can be learned.

Clara M. Maurer
Henry Shaw Cactus Society
St Louis, Missouri
USA

Winteroecereus aureispinus

FOREWORD

By John D. Lovis

Danny Schuster is perhaps as well known as a student of and enthusiast for cacti as he is in his other main field of endeavour, wine-making. He brings the same qualities of energy, enthusiasm, and a relentless drive for accuracy and increased knowledge to his new book on cacti. Danny's first book on cacti was deservedly well-received, being appreciated both for its practical approach and the quality of its copious illustrations. In *The World of Cacti* he takes the same approach, but much more ambitiously, to include descriptions and illustrations of all genera now recognised, and of more than 1000 species.

Mammillaria nana

To those who do know Danny's first book, *An Introduction to Cacti in New Zealand*, this new volume will need no recommendation beyond its author's name. I can assure those who have not seen the earlier book that they may also approach the present volume with every confidence in its contents.

John D. Lovis, BSc, PhD, DSc
Professor of Botany
Department of Plant & Microbial Sciences
University of Canterbury
Christchurch, New Zealand

Mammillaria neomystax

INTRODUCTION

Why grow cacti? This question is often asked by people seeing for the first time collections of plants resembling balls of spines displayed on the window sill, in a garden or glasshouse. Often the answer is that it is simply a matter of impulse, although to a cactus collector, no other group of flowering plants is more fascinating. Most 'cactophiles' or cactus-lovers are introduced to their hobby early in life. Usually a friend gives them an offset of an unusually fierce-looking plant with sharp spines and an exotic name like *Opuntia* or *Echinopsis*. The young recipient is unaware that a single plant will probably lead to a keen interest in an ever-growing collection of different cacti. The great adaptibility of cacti to adverse conditions, their seemingly unending variation in shape and colour, and, not least, the exotic beauty of their flowers will capture the plant-grower for life.

During the first year or so, the plant's proud owner will discover that many notions about cacti are no more than myths. In spite of popular belief, cactus spines are not poisonous, and flowering occurs with great regularity, not just every seven years. Cacti are hardy and can occupy a minimum of space and, because of their resilient nature, these remarkable plants need little attention or specialised care. A profusion of colourful flowers and spines have more than once converted a sceptic into a dedicated collector.

Given the space limitations of an average contemporary home or flat — with or without garden — the area available for growing plants is rapidly decreasing. Many of the old-fashioned, large house plants require a great deal of attention and demand conditions that are lacking in modern houses. Cacti, on the other hand, seem to thrive in adverse condi-

Pelecyphora aselliformis

tions and suffer little from lack of space or limited attention. Few, if any, plant types can match cacti in their ability to convert a small window sill into an exotic garden of shapes, rich in colour and with a profusion of flowers from mid-winter through to the heat of late summer. Possibly the most convenient aspect of growing cacti as house or office plants is that they are hardy and will survive for great lengths of time without watering. Many growers return home from a holiday of three or more weeks to find their cacti in a better shape than when they left! In fact, most cacti are more likely to be killed by kindness, for example by frequent repotting or over-watering.

The conditions and care under which most cacti will thrive are simple and easy to achieve. Once established on a sunny window sill, porch or in sheltered corner of a garden, cacti will continue to grow and flower with minimum attention. The variety of native habitats of the different cactus groups indicates that they are naturally adapted to a wide range of summer and winter conditions. Most attractive collections of cacti can be maintained in countries as diverse as Canada, the United States, Europe, Australia or New Zealand. For the professional grower or nursery-owner, cacti are ideal plants. Their ease of propagation, combined with minimal space requirements and their rapid growth to a saleable, mature plant are all great advantages.

The hybridisation of older species and new finds of cacti in the Americas provide established collectors with the continuing interest of adding to their chosen selection. A steadily growing and now widespread interest in cacti is best shown by the rapidly increasing number of cactus societies and clubs in most countries. The number of specialised nurseries in the United Kingdom, Holland, Germany, the United States, Australia, New Zealand and Japan is also increasing, providing the grower with a wide choice of plants.

Membership of a society or club provides the newcomer to the world of cacti with an opportunity to learn more about these fascinating plants — in an informal atmosphere of friendship with experienced growers — and also the opportunity to visit cactus collections all over the world. The generosity of collectors with plants and information is legendary and, like many before me, I owe a great debt of gratitude to many such hobbyists in Europe, Australia and New Zealand. Without their guidance, advice and assistance over the past twenty-five years, my own collection — and this book — would not have been possible.

I owe a debt of gratitude, as well, to Jaap Koster in New Zealand and Kasia Winiarski in the United States, both skilful photographers of plants, who applied their craft with dedication to record the fascinating beauty of cacti in collections and their native habitats. Some of the photographs are of plants from my own collection; others are from collections of experienced growers, such as the late Mr N. Stow in Christchurch, New Zealand, or have come from the well-kept slide collection of the Christchurch and New Zealand Society of Succulent and Cacti Growers, made available by Mr G. Barker, himself a notable cactus collector.

Finally, thanks to my editor, Meryl Potter, and Charles Pierson for their enthusiasm, professional skills and encouragement, which made this project such a pleasure.

D. F. Schuster
Christchurch

Mammillaria bombycina

CHAPTER 1

THE ORIGINS, CLASSIFICATION AND NATIVE HABITATS OF CACTI

Origins of Cacti

Cactus plants belong to a much larger group of plants called succulents. All of these diverse plants have adapted to arid or semi-arid conditions by modifying part or all of their structure to retain water: thickening of the leaves, body or roots of succulents are characteristic adaptations. Cacti are dicotyledonous, that is, their seedlings have two primary leaves, and their seed pod, or fruit, is a one-celled berry. All cactus flowers have petals above the seed-bearing pod, and the stigma is divided into a number of lobes. All cacti have specialised growing points, or areolae, from which spines, wool and sometimes flowers grow. Cacti are perennial: they live for a number of years and do not die after seasonal flowering and production of seeds.

In the past, during a period of more favourable climatic conditions, the natural range of cactus distribution was much greater than in more recent times. The hitherto widespread and uninterrupted distribution of related cactus genera has gradually changed to today's more isolated patterns of distribution. A cooler and less humid climate in many regions has forced the cacti to retreat. In areas where the climatic changes occurred over a long period, perhaps hundreds of thousands of years, many cacti adapted well to the change. The reduction of leaves to spines or bristles, seen in *Opuntia* and *Pereskia* species, is a good example of gradual adaptation. The loss of stems and the formation of a thickened body of rounded (globular) or columnar (cereoid) shape ensured that moisture loss is kept to a minimum. The decline in water loss because of reduced transpiration, combined with the reservoir of water stored in the modified tissues of the thickened body and roots, allow cacti to survive in the arid conditions of many parts of the Americas.

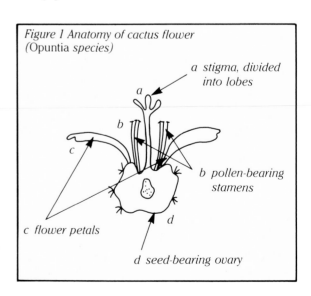

Figure 1 Anatomy of cactus flower
(Opuntia *species*)

a stigma, divided into lobes

b pollen-bearing stamens

c flower petals

d seed-bearing ovary

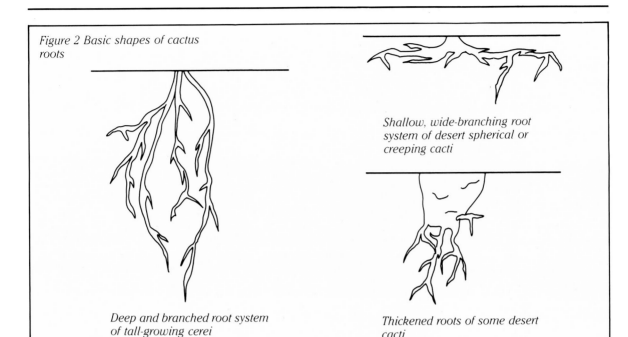

Figure 2 Basic shapes of cactus roots

Shallow, wide-branching root system of desert spherical or creeping cacti

Deep and branched root system of tall-growing cerei

Thickened roots of some desert cacti

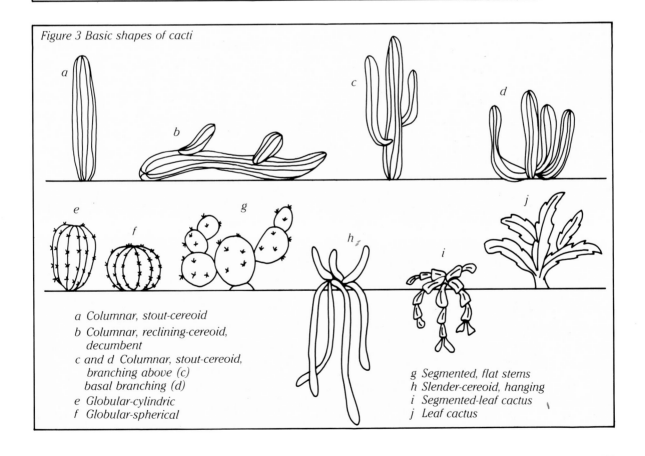

Figure 3 Basic shapes of cacti

a Columnar, stout-cereoid
b Columnar, reclining-cereoid, decumbent
c and d Columnar, stout-cereoid, branching above (c) basal branching (d)
e Globular-cylindric
f Globular-spherical

g Segmented, flat stems
h Slender-cereoid, hanging
i Segmented-leaf cactus
j Leaf cactus

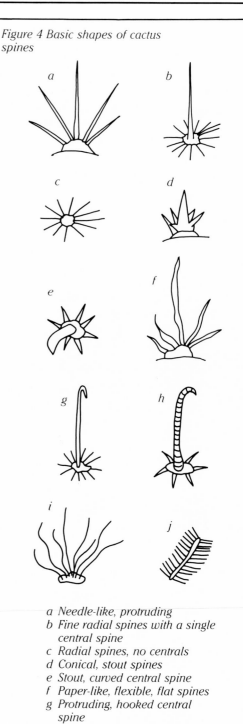

Figure 4 Basic shapes of cactus spines

a

b

c

d

e

f

g

h

i

j

a Needle-like, protruding
b Fine radial spines with a single central spine
c Radial spines, no centrals
d Conical, stout spines
e Stout, curved central spine
f Paper-like, flexible, flat spines
g Protruding, hooked central spine
h Stout, banded, curved central spine
i Bristly, hair-like spines
j Comb-like, pectinate spines

Glasshouse collection at Christchurch Botanical Gardens, New Zealand

Further marked differences in cactus genera developed as a result of dramatic changes in the landscape of their habitat, such as the rise of the Andes, which separated the ancestral cactus types of eastern South America from the Pacific branch in Chile. Furthermore, natural hybridisation, resulting from cross-fertilisation of related species of cacti, is a continuing process even today, and no doubt it will continue into the future to complicate all attempts to provide a definitive classification of all naturally occurring cacti.

The natural distribution of cacti extends from the northern limits of the United States and the Canadian border, through to Central America and the West Indies, into South America, reaching its southern limit in Brazil and Argentina. Countries in which most of the cactus genera are found include the United States, Mexico, Cuba, the West Indies, Hon-

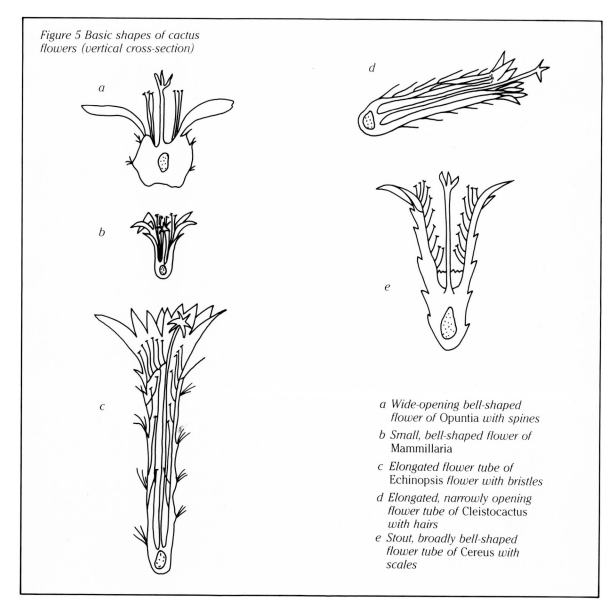

Figure 5 Basic shapes of cactus flowers (vertical cross-section)

a *Wide-opening bell-shaped flower of* Opuntia *with spines*

b *Small, bell-shaped flower of* Mammillaria

c *Elongated flower tube of* Echinopsis *flower with bristles*

d *Elongated, narrowly opening flower tube of* Cleistocactus *with hairs*

e *Stout, broadly bell-shaped flower tube of* Cereus *with scales*

duras, Chile, Bolivia, Uruguay, Paraguay, Peru, Guatemala, Ecuador, Brazil and Argentina. Figure 6 shows the widespread distribution of cacti in Americas.

Recent studies suggest that plants of the genus *Rhipsalis* found in the southern parts of Africa, Madagascar and Ceylon are native populations rather than modern introductions, as previously thought. This conclusion remains, however, controversial. The native range of the genus *Rhipsalis (Gärtner)*, namely *R. cassutha*, *R. corraloides*, *R. fasciculata*, *R. horrida*, *R. lindbergiana*, *R. madascarensis*, *R. pilosa*, *R. prismatica* and *R. saxicola* species, therefore, remains to be determined.

Classification of Cacti

All plants, including cacti, are named according to the rules of the *International Code of Botanical Nomenclature*. This code is based on the following principles:

1. any one plant can have only one valid name;
2. any one valid name can apply to only one plant;
3. the earliest validly published name for a given plant has priority over later ones; and
4. the identity of each plant named is fixed by a type specimen nominated by its author.

In practice this means that the author, that is, the person who first names the plant in question, publishes a full Latin description of the plant and gives its natural distribution.

Classifications, like that of the cactus plant family, are based on grouping like plants into units that reflect the relationship between them. The system used in botany starts with the largest grouping, the family, and proceeds through sub-family, tribe, sub-tribe and section sub-section units, to the smallest divisions of genus, species and variety. In their

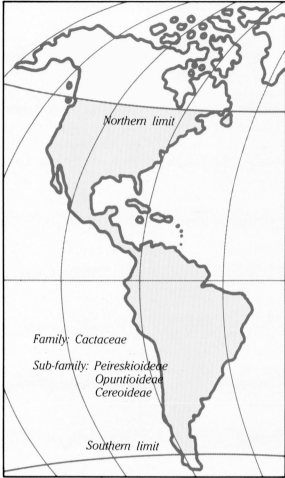

Figure 6 The distribution of cacti in their natural habitat (after Backeberg 1976)

native habitat cacti grow in groups (populations) of various size and composition of more or less related genera and species. Individual plants within each group display differences in one or more characteristics, such as body shape, spine length or flower colour. Plants of the same genus and species often occur over an extended geographical area, and local adaptations can be observed in such plants found in different locations. The task facing a botanist attempting to classify plants is to distinguish differences in plant structure that are due to local adaptations and natural variability within a species, from those that separate it from related plants. The difficulty in achieving this can be observed from the classifications of the cactus family published to date. Interpretations by different authors of classifications and cactus names are more or less in agreement as far as the larger groupings are concerned. But at the lower level of plant units, such as genus and species, major differences of opinion exist.

It would appear that, in the century or so of systematic collection and classification of cacti, two major lines of thought have emerged. Before outlining this problem further, it may be of interest to consider what the names of genus, species and variety actually represent.

A **genus** (plural genera) in botany is a subdivision of a plant family, consisting of one or more species that show similar characteristics and appear to have a common ancestry. Plants within one genus should not be readily cross-fertile with plants of another genus, whilst the chief characteristics of the genus should be genetically stable, that is, maintained after propagation from seed. The first part of the plant name — such as *Opuntia* — is the genus name.

A **species** is a group of closely related plants, bearing a group of similar characteristics that intercross freely. A species is a botanical subdivision of a genus that shows intermediate stages in any single character, such as flower, colour or spine length. A species should be distinct from all other species in the genus by a combination of characteristics. The second part of the botanical name — such as *engelmannii* in *Opuntia engelmannii* — is the specific name.

A **variety** is a group of plants within a species that share the same characteristics, but differ in minor characteristics from other groups within the species. This term is also used to indicate an improved variant of a cultivated plant, that is, a cultivar, in, for example, *Opuntia engelmannii* var. *discata*.

Different varieties within one species are usually completely infertile, and intermediate forms may be common. In practice, however, not all species are completely genetically isolated from one another, and populations of inter-specific hybrid origin, showing a range of intermediate forms, often occur in nature.

The generally acceptable outline of what constitutes genus, species and variety given above demonstrates how closely related plants at the lower end of botanical classification are, even without the complications arising from local adaptations or the naming of plants from a cultivated specimen rather than from a whole population observed in its native habitat. Various authors of cactus names and classifications have differed, and no doubt still differ today, on the interpretation of the naturally occurring divergences in morphological characters seen in otherwise uniform populations of like plants within one location, or locations some distance apart. Sometimes new genera have been named (unwisely) after only a single character divergence has been observed, such as the presence of bristles at the base of flower tube, or the length of the flower tube, or the length of spines. To a more conservative botanist, a single character as such is no more important than any other single characteristic. The importance of a single characteristic as a marker of a genus, species or any other botanical category is only in proportion to its degree of consistency of association with other characters. The value of even accurate observations made on a single plant in a collection, far from its natural habitat or in a herbarium, is limited, but, on the other hand, studies of natural populations of plants, where intermediate stages of morphological characters can be seen more clearly, are often difficult to accomplish. It is easy to see how a single plant in different locations could receive more than one name. The widespread use of a popular name, such as cholla for plants of the genus *Opuntia*, can be also misleading, as the name often covers a whole group of more or less related genera.

Authors of cactus books differ in their acceptance of particular generic or specific names for cacti, partly according to practicality and partly to the prevailing fashion of the time in botanical circles. Before the Second World War, and to a lesser degree during 1950s and 1960s, the prevailing trend in classifying cacti led to a proliferation of new genera and species. More recently, the tendency has changed toward increasing the use of sub-specific and varietal names, and to drastically reducing the number of genera and species in modern classifications of cacti.

Boojum tree (*Cirio* species) in the Sonora Desert in Arizona

Both tendencies arise from the desire to classify cacti in a uniform and consistent manner, and in that they are both right. The principal difference between the two trends lies in the interpretation of what constitutes a divergent, morphological character and how important such a character is, compared with other characteristics that remain the same. Many systematic classifications of the cactus family published to date, such as works by Britton and Rose (1922), Buxbaum (1956), Backeberg (1966), Ritter (1972) and Götz (1984), show the differences of opinion that exist, though for a collector of cacti this may prove of little importance. The more specialised cactus collector, interested in a single group of genera from a geographically well-defined area, will no doubt be guided by the more specialised literature published on the subject, such as the treatise of W. Rausch on *Lobivia* (1975), Brinkmann's on *Sulcorebutia* (1976) or L. Benson's *Cacti of Arizona* (1977).

This text attempts to give the reader an overall understanding of the major groups of cactus genera that form the Cactaceae family, rather than adding to already complex problems of cactus classification. The cactus types selected do not include all the genera found in nature. The plants selected are largely those found in collections, those that can be obtained, and those whose body, flowers and spination make them attractive.

As will be seen from the descriptions that follow, a certain amount of specialised, botanical terminology has had to be included, but the use of Latin names has been kept to a minimum. In all cases the nomenclature has been restricted to names in common use and to those that are generally accepted by growers and nursery-owners. Where significant differences of opinion exist, these are referred to in the text to provide a reader with an overall appreciation of the various schools of thought, rather than to provide a definitive guide to individual names.

Cholla (*Opuntia*) in Joshua National Monument in Arizona,   Barrel cactus (*Ferocactus* species) in background

Both the name of the genus and species are included in that order, such as *Gymnocalycium multiflorum*. The standard formal botanical practice of including the author's name(s) in brackets after each plant's name is not followed here for the sake of brevity. It is, however, acknowledged that the collector's name and the plant's field number, if available from a supplier of seed, should be included on labels of plants and seed collected in the wild to make individual plant identification easier, for example, *Acanthocalycium glaucum FR 970.** This practice would be helpful to all growers and collectors, as plants could thus be readily identified, despite variations in classifications that may be in use at any one time. A full list of genera and species included in the illustrated section of this book is given at the beginning of chapter 4.

*Field number and the initials of the author's name that sometimes follow the name of a cactus genus or species refer to a number given to a plant by its collector. For example the above plant collected by Friedrich Ritter in Argentina's province of Catamarca and described in Taxon, XIII:4, 143 in 1964 was given a field number FR 970. Since that time this cactus has been known to collectors as *Acanthocalycium glaucum FR 970.*

BOTANICAL CLASSIFICATION OF THE CACTACEAE FAMILY OF PLANTS

(after C. Backeberg 1976)

All genera are in italics

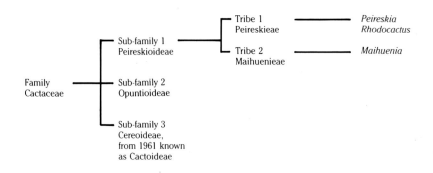

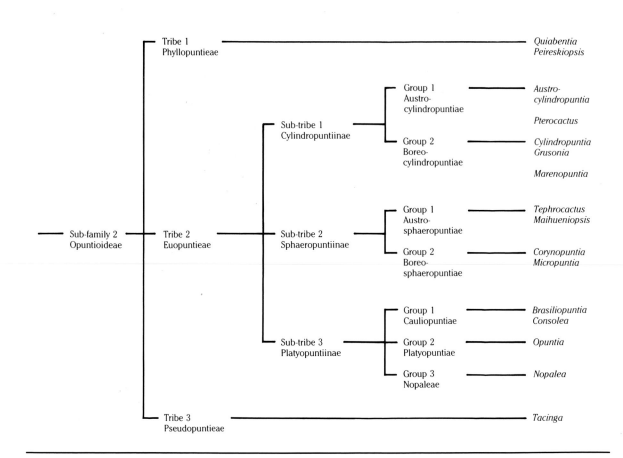

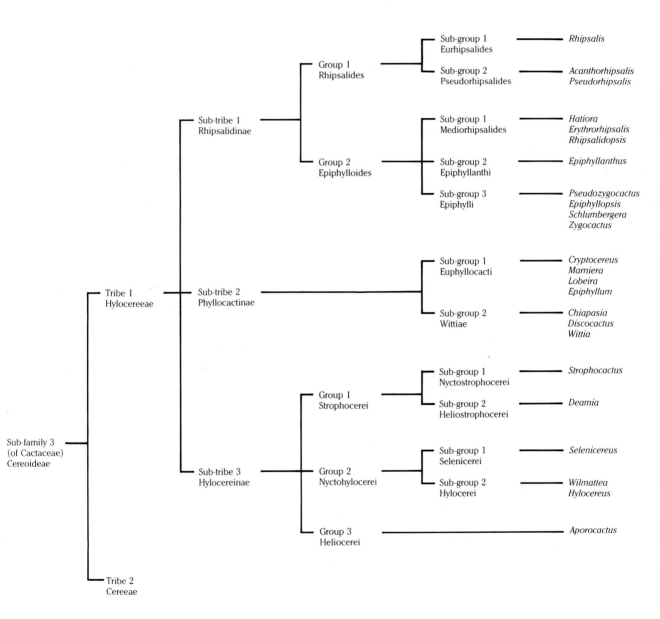

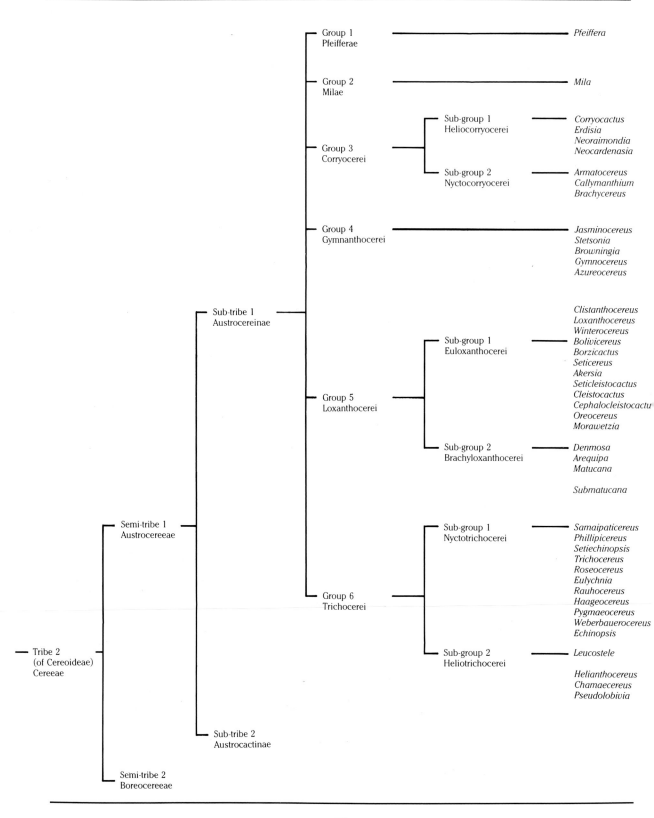

		Group 1 Pfeifferae			*Pfeiffera*
		Group 2 Milae			*Mila*
		Group 3 Corryocerei	Sub-group 1 Heliocorryocerei		*Corryocactus* *Erdisia* *Neoraimondia* *Neocardenasia*
			Sub-group 2 Nyctocorryocerei		*Armatocereus* *Callymanthium* *Brachycereus*
		Group 4 Gymnanthocerei			*Jasminocereus* *Stetsonia* *Browningia* *Gymnocereus* *Azureocereus*

Sub-tribe 1
Austrocereinae

Group 5
Loxanthocerei

Sub-group 1
Euloxanthocerei

Clistanthocereus
Loxanthocereus
Winterocereus
Bolivicereus
Borzicactus
Seticereus
Akersia
Seticleistocactus
Cleistocactus
Cephalocleistocactu
Oreocereus
Morawetzia

Sub-group 2
Brachyloxanthocerei

Denmosa
Arequipa
Matucana

Submatucana

Semi-tribe 1
Austrocereeae

Group 6
Trichocerei

Sub-group 1
Nyctotrichocerei

Samaipaticereus
Phillipicereus
Setiechinopsis
Trichocereus
Roseocereus
Eulychnia
Rauhocereus
Haageocereus
Pygmaeocereus
Weberbauerocereus
Echinopsis

Tribe 2
(of Cereoideae)
Cereeae

Sub-group 2
Heliotrichocerei

Leucostele

Helianthocereus
Chamaecereus
Pseudolobivia

Sub-tribe 2
Austrocactinae

Semi-tribe 2
Boreocereeae

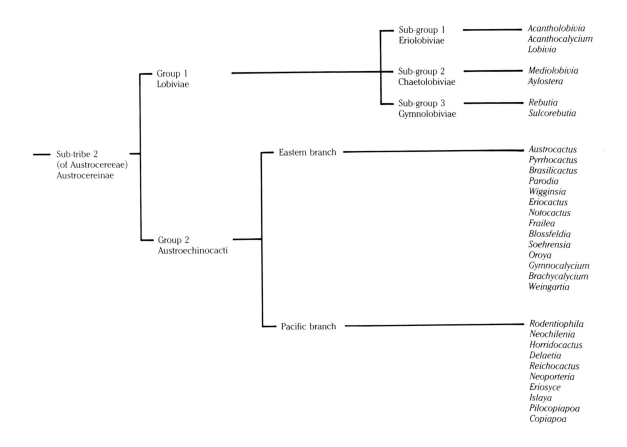

- Sub-tribe 2 (of Austrocereeae) Austrocereinae
  - Group 1 Lobiviae
    - Sub-group 1 Eriolobiviae — *Acantholobivia* *Acanthocalycium* *Lobivia*
    - Sub-group 2 Chaetolobiviae — *Mediolobivia* *Aylostera*
    - Sub-group 3 Gymnolobiviae — *Rebutia* *Sulcorebutia*
  - Group 2 Austroechinocacti
    - Eastern branch — *Austrocactus* *Pyrrhocactus* *Brasilicactus* *Parodia* *Wigginsia* *Eriocactus* *Notocactus* *Frailea* *Blossfeldia* *Soehrensia* *Oroya* *Gymnocalycium* *Brachycalycium* *Weingartia*
    - Pacific branch — *Rodentiophila* *Neochilenia* *Horridocactus* *Delaetia* *Reichocactus* *Neoporteria* *Eriosyce* *Islaya* *Pilocopiapoa* *Copiapoa*

Dense scrubland (chapparal) in Tucson Valley, Arizona

Ocotilla bush (*Fouquiera splendens*) in the grasslands of Arizona

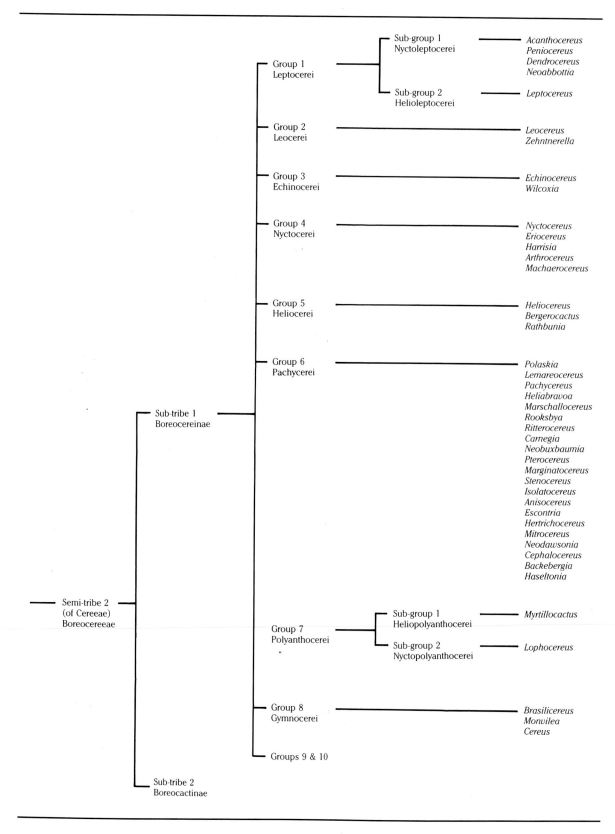

Group 1
Leptocerei

Sub-group 1
Nyctoleptocerei

Acanthocereus
Peniocereus
Dendrocereus
Neoabbottia

Sub-group 2
Helioleptocerei

Leptocereus

Group 2
Leocerei

Leocereus
Zehntnerella

Group 3
Echinocerei

Echinocereus
Wilcoxia

Group 4
Nyctocerei

Nyctocereus
Eriocereus
Harrisia
Arthrocereus
Machaerocereus

Group 5
Heliocerei

Heliocereus
Bergerocactus
Rathbunia

Group 6
Pachycerei

Polaskia
Lemareocereus
Pachycereus
Heliabravoa
Marschallocereus
Rooksbya
Ritterocereus
Carnegia
Neobuxbaumia
Pterocereus
Marginatocereus
Stenocereus
Isolatocereus
Anisocereus
Escontria
Hertrichocereus
Mitrocereus
Neodawsonia
Cephalocereus
Backebergia
Haseltonia

Sub-tribe 1
Boreocereinae

Semi-tribe 2
(of Cereeae)
Boreocereeae

Group 7
Polyanthocerei

Sub-group 1
Heliopolyanthocerei

Myrtillocactus

Sub-group 2
Nyctopolyanthocerei

Lophocereus

Group 8
Gymnocerei

Brasilicereus
Monvilea
Cereus

Groups 9 & 10

Sub-tribe 2
Boreocactinae

22

Glasshouse collection at Christchurch Botanical Gardens, New Zealand

Glasshouse collection at Christchurch Botanical Gardens, New Zealand

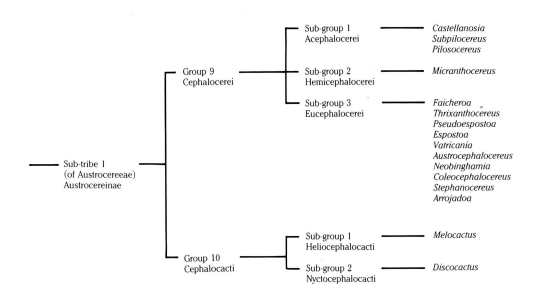

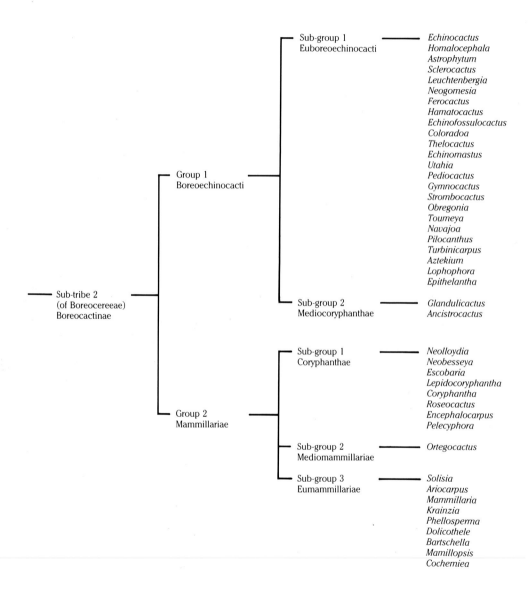

Sub-group 1
Euboreoechinocacti

Echinocactus
Homalocephala
Astrophytum
Sclerocactus
Leuchtenbergia
Neogomesia
Ferocactus
Hamatocactus
Echinofossulocactus
Coloradoa
Thelocactus
Echinomastus
Utahia
Pediocactus
Gymnocactus
Strombocactus
Obregonia
Tourneya
Navajoa
Pilocanthus
Turbinicarpus
Aztekium
Lophophora
Epithelantha

Group 1
Boreoechinocacti

Sub-group 2
Mediocoryphanthae

Glandulicactus
Ancistrocactus

Sub-tribe 2
(of Boreocereeae)
Boreocactinae

Sub-group 1
Coryphanthae

Neolloydia
Neobesseya
Escobaria
Lepidocoryphantha
Coryphantha
Roseocactus
Encephalocarpus
Pelecyphora

Group 2
Mammillariae

Sub-group 2
Mediomammillariae

Ortegocactus

Sub-group 3
Eumammillariae

Solisia
Ariocarpus
Mammillaria
Krainzia
Phellosperma
Dolicothele
Bartschella
Mamillopsis
Cochemiea

Opuntia violacea var. *santa-rosa* in grasslands of southern Arizona

Natural Habitats of Cacti

A general outline of the major cactus habitats in South and North America should provide a basic understanding of the environments under which cacti grow in nature. Duplicating these conditions as far as possible will contribute to successful culture of cacti indoors, in the glasshouse or in the garden.

TRUE DESERT

This habitat consists of the truly dry, arid regions, where exceedingly low rainfall of less than 100 millimetres a year limits vegetation to low-growing, usually prostrate plants that are specially modified to withstand extreme conditions of heat and cold. Desert environment is typified by low, irregular rainfall, low soil fertility and soils of high stone and low humus content. True desert climate is characterised by contrasting night and day temperatures, from near chilling point at night to extreme heat during the day, giving a range of up to 50 Celsius degrees.

Cactus types found in true deserts are the small, globular (rounded) plants growing in clumps, or the low, cereoid (columnar) types growing in prostrate fashion. Both of these forms are well adapted to a short growing season and minimum water loss. Much of the moisture available in the desert is in the form of morning dew and spring rainfall, so plants have adapted toward a shallow, densely branched root system that allows rapid uptake of water. In addition, spination points downward, directing water toward the base of each plant.

Cacti in the Mojave Desert in Arizona

Some low-growing *Opuntia* and *Echinocereus* species are good examples of desert cacti found in the south-western United States. The simple rosette-shaped body of *Ariocarpus* from central Mexico is another example of the adaptation of cacti to desert conditions. Other flora found in deserts include the creosote bush (*Larrea divaricata*) in the Mexican desert, ocotilla bush (*Fouquieria splendens*) in the Arizona desert, the smoke tree (*Dalea spinosa*) in the Colorado desert and the Joshua tree (*Yucca brevifolia*) in the Mojavean desert. Only rarely is any one species of cactus confined to a single type habitat, although concentrations of plant population will be greater in preferred positions. An example of this tendency is the presence of numerous populations of saguaro cactus (*Cereus giganteus*) at higher elevations of the Arizona desert and the concentrations of *Sclerocactus* and *Pediocactus* species in the Navajoan desert.

DESERT GRASSLANDS

These are arid to semi-arid regions, often bordering deserts. Like deserts, they are typified by low rainfall and sparse vegetation, which is restricted to various grasses and low-growing bushes. Depending on elevation above sea level and topography, the number of genera and species of cactus increases to a point where cacti dominate the local flora or grow in highly localised populations. Many of the cacti of North and South America thrive in these conditions, in south-eastern Arizona, southern New Mexico and Mojave county in the United States, northern Mexico, Chile and the higher elevations of the eastern Andes in Bolivia and Argentina.

Well-drained soils, with a high stone content, winters of low temperatures and rainfall, and high summer temperatures are typical. The humus content of the soil tends to be higher than in true deserts, whilst the moisture content and salinity of the uppermost soil layer are reduced.

Cereus giganteus in open scrublands of western Tucson Valley, Arizona

Many species of *Ferocacti*, *Mammillaria*, *Opuntia*, *Neolloydia*, *Coryphantha* and related genera are found in the desert grasslands of North America; *Gymnocalycium* and many *Lobivia* or *Copiapoa* species grow under similar conditions in South America.

LOW BUSHLANDS OR CHAPARRALS

These environments, in which greater depth of soil and increased rainfall allow a more or less continuous bush cover, enable some of the more sensitive species of cactus to survive in numbers, with partial or full protection from the sun. Depending on the topography and geographical position of a region, cacti in bushlands receive more water during the growing season, and the winter–summer and day–night temperature variations are greatly reduced. Species such as those of the genera *Mammillaria*, *Astrophythum*, some *Opuntias*, *Cereus* and *Echinocereus* are found in bushlands of North America; some species of *Notocactus*, *Eriocactus*, *Cleistocactus*, *Parodia* and *Trichocereus* are found in similar habitats in South America.

SUBTROPICAL FORESTS

These are warm, humîd regions of Central America, the West Indies, and Brazil, where numerous epiphytic and climbing cacti grow. Using the branches or trunks of trees for support, these cacti demand warm, sheltered positions with an ample supply of water during growing and flowering. In great contrast to the arid to semi-arid habitats, forest environments are typified by warm, humid conditions, soils that are both fertile and rich in humus, and regular supplies of water and diffused light.

Numerous species of *Melocacti*, *Rhipsalis*, climbing *Cerei*, *Monvillea*, *Selenicereus*, *Epiphyllum* and *Rhipsalidopsis* are found in this environment. Their requirements for water, protection from full sun, and mild winter temperatures, as well as increased air humidity and fertile soil, are all related to the conditions of their habitat.

Sunrise in southern Arizona

Typical landscape in Saguaro National Monument in Arizona

Examples of topographical and climatic data from natural habitats of cacti in North and South America (after *World Atlas of Climate* 1967)

Region	Altitude above sea level (metres)	Annual mean temperature (°Celsius)	Annual rainfall (millimetres)	Frost incidence
Tucson (Arizona)	420	19.5	293 (w)*	Yes
Chihuahua (Mexico)	1423	18.1	394 (s)*	Yes
Durango (Mexico)	1889	17.1	484 (s)	Yes
Zacatecas (Mexico)	2612	13.1	365 (s)	Yes
San Louis Potosi (Mexico)	1377	17.6	361 (s)	Yes
Leon (Mexico)	1809	18.8	660 (s)	Yes
Queretaro (Mexico)	1853	17.8	508 (s)	Yes
Mexico city (Mexico)	2280	15.6	588 (s)	No
La Paz (S. California)	18	24.5	173 (w)	No
Lima (Peru)	158	19.3	48 (w)	No
Taltal (Chile)	39	17.3	11	No
Coquimbo (Chile)	27	14.6	114 (w)	No
Arequipa (Peru)	2451	13.8	106 (s)	No
Cajamarca (Peru)	2810	14.6	1144 (s)	No
Cochabamba (Bolivia)	2575	17.3	462 (s)	No
Potosi (Bolivia)	2850	12.4	665 (s)	No
Jujuy (Argentina)	1270	17.0	743 (s)	No
Salta (Argentina)	1220	17.5	712 (s)	No
Tucuman (Argentina)	481	19.1	974 (s)	No
Catamarca (Argentina)	547	20.5	357 (s)	No
Montes Claros (Brazil)	615	21.8	1247 (s)	No
Parana (Argentina)	65	18.8	876 (s)	No
Rio de Janeiro (Brazil)	60	23.2	1099 (s)	No
Santos (Brazil)	3	21.9	2084 (s + w)	No

Notes: *S = mainly summer
*W = mainly winter

CHAPTER 2

SUITABLE ENVIRONMENTS FOR GROWING CACTI

The wide-ranging variations of soil types and climates that form the natural habitats for cacti demonstrate the extreme adaptibility of these remarkable plants. The cereoid (columnar), globular (rounded) or epiphytic (segmented) cacti are found in arid deserts, the desert grasslands of the United States, Chile and Mexico, and the seemingly inhospitable mountain slopes of the Andes, as well as the subtropical forests of Brazil. Cactus species in all these environments have adapted to survive, so the best conditions for successful culture of cacti indoors or in the garden duplicate the major soil and climatic characteristics of the cactus's native habitat.

Unless specifically stated otherwise, as for *Zygocactus* or *Melocactus* for example, the cacti selected for this text will grow and flower well given the following cultivation conditions:

1. a coarse soil mix that allows rapid water drainage and easy root penetration;

2. a soil type that has slightly acidic pH reaction, low humus content, and an ample supply of potassium and phosphorus;

3. a position with plentiful sun and warmth, even for only part of the day, combined with regular watering during active growth and flowering;

4. a cool and dry rest period with no watering, during the inactive winter months; lack of moisture during the winter months can be tempered by misting the plants with water on fine days;

5. a basic protection from excessive heat in glasshouses, overheating of roots of potted plants, or frosts in cold climate regions; and

6. prevention of mould and insect infestations.

More detailed conditions for cultivating cacti under glass, indoors or in open gardens are given below.

Light

Under outdoor conditions, most cacti are best suited to full light and a sunny position. Many genera are well adapted to thrive in conditions of great light intensity and summer heat. Fine wool, dense spines and deeply carved ribs act as a protection against the sun's rays and excessive light. A sheltered verandah, or the sun-exposed corner of a garden are well suited to duplicating natural conditions.

Covering garden soil around the base of plants with a light-coloured coarse gravel will reflect much of the light received and will also ensure that the soil near the plants is kept dry. Cacti will thrive better under the harsher summer conditions of an outdoor garden. Their growth will be slower, but more sturdy; plants will flower more freely; and they will withstand greater amounts of direct sun without damage from sunburn. Plants raised and grown indoors, or in glasshouses, will grow

Stand of *Cereus giganteus* in grasslands of Saguaro National Monument in Arizona, with a silver cholla (*Opuntia echinocarpa*) in the foreground

faster and have a better appearance, but they will also be more sensitive to sunburn during the hot periods of mid-summer.

An excessive build-up of heat in glass-covered areas can be avoided by shading and regular ventilation. The brown scarring of the surface tissues of cacti is caused by excessive sunlight and heat and, although this rarely damages older plants, it can make them less attractive.

On the other hand, insufficient light will cause cacti to display pale coloration and result in an elongation of the growing tip and poor flowering. Forced winter growth — caused by excessive warmth and winter watering — should be avoided, except for young seedlings, which are best raised in a glass-house under improved or supplemented light.

The subtropical, epiphytic cacti (such as *Schlumbergera, Zygocactus*) favour semi-shade during the period of summer growth. The required dispersed light and less intense heat, combined with greater humidity, can be found under the branches of larger trees, partly covered verandahs or similar locations. The large and colourful flowers of these tropical cacti will develop best on the hardened, well-coloured segments, which have, under open-air conditions, had a chance to mature in the semi-shade.

Conditions of more or less constant heat and good light intensity will support flowering in the cooler months of the year. Sudden changes of temperature, moisture and light, will often result in flower-bud drop or poor coloration of flowers.

All cactus seedlings should be shielded from full sun until they have developed spines to provide protection. Some genera, for example *Gymnocalycium* and *Parodia*, will benefit from slightly shaded positions. The flowering of such cacti in glasshouses will be improved by placing them in a cool position away from direct sunlight. In the generally cooler conditions of a garden, shade will be less critical.

Temperature

In their natural environment of North and South America, cacti experience a temperature range typified by cool, dry winters and warm springs. Spring rains are followed by dry, hot summers, and the growing cycle for most varieties of cactus reflect these conditions. Cacti are well adapted to gain the maximum advantage from any water available during the spring, and this results in a rapid swelling of the body and the appearance of flowers. During the hot part of the summer, cacti retain moisture in their tissues for long periods. Shrivelling and reduced tension in body-surface tissue minimises moisture loss, and the combination of spines and hair or wool provides shade from direct sunlight.

Winters are usually cold and dry. Some genera of catus (such as *Cereus* and *Espostoa*) are found in areas with winter frost, although, with decreasing temperature, their resistance to excess moisture in the soil and atmosphere is decreased. Also, under natural conditions, cactus plants undergo a period of hardening in late summer and autumn. Under the artificial conditions of cultivation, the growing season is extended well into autumn, and it is important to assist the hardening of plants by reducing the frequency of watering, and by ensuring adequate ventilation at night.

Hardened plants will be better able to withstand the colder winter months. In districts with severe winter frosts (−3°C or greater), further protection from frost may be required. Glasshouse plants can benefit from improved insulation and limited heating, outdoor plants

from being covered or brought indoors. In areas with severe winters (northern Europe, Canada), plants are often taken out of the soil and stored, carefully wrapped in paper for protection, and placed inside boxes. Cacti in these conditions can be kept in the cool, dry environment of a cellar until the warmer months of spring, when they are repotted and placed in their summer position (figure 7).

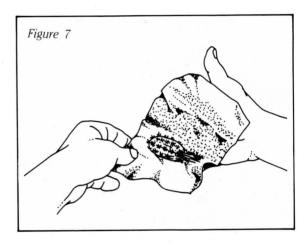

Figure 7

Some larger specimens of columnar cacti grown in gardens (such as *Trichocereus* and *Oreocereus*) can withstand mild frosts without damage, providing the roots and the base of each plant are dry. Covering the soil and the base of the plant with mulched straw provides a suitable frost protection. Outdoor cacti planted in positions exposed to winter rain have a low tolerance to winter frosts.

The over-heating of poorly ventilated glasshouses can cause brown scarring in cacti and, except on wet or cold days, ventilators should be kept open during summer and autumn. Frequent ventilation of glasshouses during fine, sunny days in winter is also recommended, to avoid a build-up of stale air, which could favour the spread of insect infestations and mould. Excessive heat and moisture build-up in glasshouses during winter could also lead to premature winter growth, and to cacti having distorted shapes.

Moisture and Watering

Regular watering should be restricted to the months when there is visible, active growth of plants. In principle, watering to 'run-off point' once or twice a week is better than watering daily. Soils should be given time to dry out between watering, rather than being kept wet. Water should be applied carefully to the soil surface, keeping the body of the cactus dry. Morning watering is preferable, though late afternoon is also suitable, providing that the soil surface has time to dry out before the cool part of the evening. Watering during the greatest heat of the day should be avoided. If it becomes necessary, humidity can safely be increased by plant misting or spraying water over the glasshouse floor.

Problems associated with excessive heat and humidity rarely arise with plants grown in a suitable part of a garden, or on a window sill or porch. Watering patterns in such positions should resemble those outlined for glasshouses — the soil again being allowed to dry out between waterings. Potted cacti will require more regular watering than plants grown in larger volumes of soil in gardens or soil-filled benches.

In the early spring it is safer not to water cacti until there is some visible growth of shiny tips, new spines or flower buds.

Freshly potted plants should not be watered until the roots have had time to grow, usually a week or two after planting. Obvious growth is again a safe indicator of the need to water.

Towards the end of the growing season, watering should be gradually decreased until the plants are hardened sufficiently for their dry, winter rest. Watering can be stopped altogether during the winter and the occasional misting of plants will prove sufficient to avoid shrivelling. Shrivelling has no detrimental or lasting effect on cacti. It is caused by gradual moisture loss and can be rapidly reversed in the spring. Plants that have not been allowed to shrivel excessively during the winter appear more attractive and begin their active growth and flowering earlier in the spring.

Water used for cacti should, ideally, have a slightly acid pH reaction, be close to air temperature and have an abundance of dissolved oxygen. These conditions can be achieved by storing rain water. When this is not convenient, tap water, with its usually high pH value (alkaline), can be suitably adjusted by adding a few drops of sulphuric acid, using litmus paper as an indicator; acid and litmus paper kits can be obtained from a chemist's shop. The litmus paper shows, by simple changes in colour, the pH value of the water which is being tested. The acid is then added, drop by drop, until the required neutral range is attained.

Soil Mix and Fertilisers

Many growers prepare their own 'special' soil mix, and opinions vary as to which mix is ideal for this or that type of cactus. Despite differing opinions, the more successful growers use a soil that drains well, thus is coarse; warms readily in the sun; allows for easy root penetration and repotting; contains low levels of nitrogen; and has balanced levels of other nutrients. In texture, suitable soil mixes range from coarse, medium coarse, medium coarse enriched with humus, to fine, the last being best suited to seedlings. A humus-enriched, medium coarse mix is often used for the tropical, epiphytic types sometimes called 'orchid cacti' (such as *Zygocactus*). Moss can be added to this mix to improve its moisture-holding capability, thus making it suitable for use in hanging baskets.

FINE SOIL MIX

A propagating mixture, which usually consists of one part sharp sand (crushed gravel, not fine beach sand) to two parts well-matured, sieved compost from peat or leaf mulch. When steamed or chemically sterilised, this fine textured soil is best suited to raising

Organ pipe cactus (*Cereus thurberî*) in open scrubland of western Pima County, Arizona

coarse soil mix, without humus enrichment, may be made from peat (30 per cent), roughly sieved garden soil, or mature leaf mulch (30 per cent) and coarse gravel or crushed brick (40 per cent). A handful of inorganic fertiliser (granulated, slow-release types are preferable), rich in potassium and phosphorus, may be added to each 10 kilogram bag of mix. Small amounts of Paradichlor-benzene crystals, as a protection against root mealy bug, can also be added (see chapter 3).

As the trade names and composition of fertilisers vary from place to place, consult a local supplier or nursery for details of the most suitable types available.

To increase the humus and moisture retention of this soil — for growing epiphytic cacti — halve the quantity of coarse gravel or crushed brick and substitute an equal amount (20 per cent) of sphagnum moss or well-composed peat moss.

COARSE SOIL MIX

This is a suitable blend for all Mexican or American desert cacti of spherical shape, or for the small, slow-growing genera from Chile, Argentina and Bolivia. The coarse soil texture will allow for a rapid drainage of water and, depending on the container used, the frequency of summer watering will be increased. A coarse soil mix may be made up from coarse gravel or crushed brick (50 per cent), peat (25 per cent) and roughly sieved, mature compost (leaf mulch 25 per cent). A handful (250–300 grams) of inorganic fertiliser, as described for medium coarse soils, should be added for each 10 kilograms of soil mix. Mealy bug protection crystals, as before, are also used.

Hydroponic* Culture and Soils

The raising of young plants — and the maintaining of larger collections — under conditions of hydroponic culture have advantages compared with more traditional methods. Hydroponic culture is best suited to larger,

young cactus seedlings or growing small plants. Usually no fertiliser is required, as sufficient nutrients for early growth are already present. Some commercial growers use nitrogen-rich fertilisers during watering, or in the form of a spray to speed-up the growth of young seedlings. Caution is advised, however, as, without experience, this procedure can lead to distortions of plant shape, insufficient hardening of tissues, and plant loss (see chapter 3).

MEDIUM COARSE SOIL MIX, WITH OR WITHOUT HUMUS ENRICHMENT

A good composition suitable for most of the taller, vigorously growing cacti (such as *Cereoid, Lobivoid, Opuntia*). It is also used for plants with a stout tap root (*Copiapoa*, some *Mammillaria* and similar genera). A medium

commercial nurseries or to cactus collectors — to conditions where detailed and continuous attention can be given to plant health and nutrition.

Hydroponic culture basically consists of a large raised bed that has been filled with inert soil, sharp sand, and crushed brick (gravel), through which a solution of nutrients is circulated at regular intervals. Young seedlings may be placed in such raised beds at an early stage and can be removed, potted and sold, when they reach a mature size.

A combination of ideal nutrients and disease control results in a more rapid development of young plants and an excellent success rate with seedlings. The expense of setting up a hydroponic bench deters many small growers and private collectors, despite the fact that hydroponic culture saves considerable time and money, which can otherwise be spent on repotting and on new soil mixes.

Hydroponic benches also create much safer conditions for raising seedlings and for maintaining mature plants.

When large collections of cacti are grown on a hydroponic bench, it is advisable to group together plants with similar moisture and nutrient requirements or, at least, to separate plants with differing growing cycles onto separate parts of the bench. The placement of cacti with regard of their future growth is also important, as this will avoid the need to re-establish grown plants at a later stage.

A typical hydroponic bench (see figure 8) could consist of a raised bed — with sides of sufficient depth to accommodate seedlings (20–25 centimetres), or mature plants (40–50 centimetres) — constructed from permanent, non-corrosive materials. Drainage outlets from the bottom of the bench may be connect-

ed by plastic piping to a container of nutrient solution below the bench.

The raised bed is filled with fine gravel or a similar inert medium, and a nutrient solution is supplied to the mix by a small pump, which pipes the liquid from a reservoir. The reservoir, which has a predetermined capacity sufficient for its purpose, is kept below the bench. The nutrients are supplied to each plant, or section of the bench, by a network of small plastic tubes, which provide 'drip feed' delivery.

Surplus nutrient solution is drained back into the reservoir and recycled for further use. It is important that the nutrient solution is checked periodically and adjusted, if necessary, to the correct strength.

Various hydroponic solutions, with a balanced nutrient content of low pH value, are suitable. In some countries already prepared solutions are available.

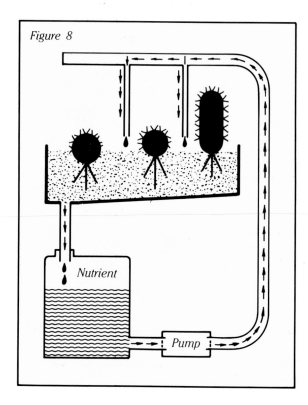

Figure 8

Nutrient

Pump

---

*Although the term hydroponic is used throughout, it should be realised that all references are to a semi-hydroponic condition, consisting of growing media — for example gravel — and a hydroponic, nutrient solution.

Generally, cacti will grow well in solutions containing equal amounts of nitrogen, potassium and phosphorus, to which amounts of minor nutrients have been added. For the best results, discuss your likely requirements with a local nursery or fertiliser supplier, and obtain detailed advice on the solutions and inorganic fertilisers available in your area.

Containers

Clay pots have traditionally been used for cacti. More recently, lighter and cheaper plastic pots have come to be used for solitary plants or for mini-gardens. The advantages of non-porous, plastic pots or painted metal tins include a reduction in moisture loss and a more even distribution of root systems throughout the available soil.

It should be remembered that containers used for cactus plants should never be excessively large and that yearly repotting of rapidly growing plants is preferable to the use of outsized pots. Frequent repotting of young plants will speed up their development, and pots of two-to-three times the diameter of the young plant are sufficient to maintain healthy growth. Mature, full-sized plants should be repotted less frequently, and usually only into pots of the same or a slightly larger size. When metal tins are used, they should be painted with a non-toxic paint to prevent rust.

Larger containers and trays can be used successfully to create mini-gardens. Four to six different cacti are usually planted together in such gardens. The contrast between the shapes and colours of plants can be complemented by the use of driftwood or other natural objects (such as stones or gravel) to isolate individual plants and generally enhance visual appeal. The positioning of taller cacti at the back and smaller, globular plants at the front allows for future plant growth and for a greater visual impact. If plants have been correctly spaced, the need for frequent repotting may be avoided and mini-gardens can be grown for a number of years in the same container.

Planting and Replanting

Before placing a plant in a pot or a tray, fill the base of the container with coarse gravel to cover the drainage hole so that excess water can escape with relative freedom (see figure 9). Hold the plant in position and add sufficient soil to the container to cover the roots of the plant to the point where they join the body. To protect the plant's spines, and the grower's hands, rolled paper or a piece of cloth may be used to hold the plant in position (see figure 10).

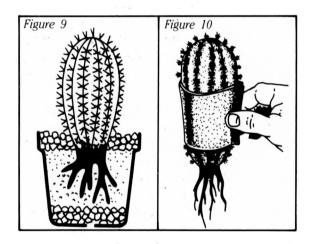

Figure 9   Figure 10

After gently firming the soil near the plant and at the edge of the container, add coarse gravel to cover the soil and the base of the plant. When removing a plant from an old container, during repotting or for any other reason, take care not to disturb the ball of roots to any great degree. Dead or diseased roots should be cut off with a sharp knife.

Growing in Large Trays and on Benches

Grouping a collection of plants in large trays or on raised benches can have advantages over the more conventional growing of cacti in pots or other small containers. In addition to the increased visual appeal of grouped plants, with different colours and shapes growing naturally rather than in isolation, repotting, maintenance and the need for frequent watering are greatly reduced.

With selective arrangement, the taller, columnar types towards the back and the smaller, globular varieties to the front, the plants should have enough space to reach three or four times their original planting size. The spaces between the plants can be filled with stones, driftwood, or similar decorative

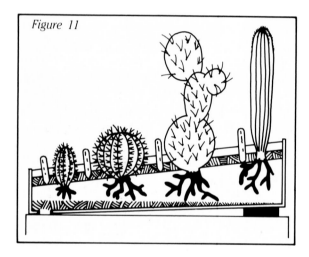

Figure 11

objects that blend with their surroundings. Under these conditions it is only necessary to repot plants every seven to ten years (see figure 11).

Some important points to remember when planting and maintaining a large cactus garden include the following:

1. Ensure that the bench supports are strong enough to carry the full weight of soil, plants and stones.
2. Make sure that the planting depth of the tray or bench allows for the development of a strong root system. A minimum of 30–50 centimetres depth will probably be required.
3. Ensure that all trays and benches are constructed from permanent, non-corrosive materials such as wood, plastic or painted metal.
4. Provide for adequate water by ensuring that the drainage holes are sited in the lowest parts of the bench or tray. Slightly elevate (3–5°) the rear support section to assist rapid drainage.
5. Remember that, when filling a bench with soil mix, a layer of gravel 5 centimetres deep at the base will assist drainage. A further layer of gravel may then be placed on top of the soil after planting to keep the plants dry and free from soil splashing during watering. The mix customarily used is a medium coarse type, which suits most cacti. A dressing of inorganic fertiliser can be added each year at the time of spring watering.
6. Delay any watering of the planted bench until the plants show visible signs of growth. Watering is then maintained during the spring and summer months at weekly to ten-day intervals, depending on plant growth and variations in temperature. Allow the soil to dry out between waterings, and avoid splashing the plants. Water should be applied gently to the gravel covering of the soil until run-off is observed from the drainage holes. During the winter, on sunny days, use a fine misting of water to avoid excessive shrivelling of mature plants.
7. Pre-determine which types of cacti go best together to give the greatest possible contrast in shape and colour of the body, spines and flowers.
8. Place small plastic or metal labels near each plant for easy identification.

Growing on Window Sills or in Plant Stands

Their hardy nature and small size make many cacti suitable for cultivation in the restricted

Figure 12

space of a window sill or on a small plant stand. Their distinctive appearance contrasts well with other house plants.

Ideal indoor positions will provide:

1. plenty of light with direct exposure to the sun for at least a few hours each day;
2. easy access to individual plants for watering during the growth period;
3. a cool position with good exposure to light during the winter months;
4. enough space, if required, to accommodate trays or larger pots planted as mini-gardens to produce a greater visual effect with several cacti grouped together; and
5. protection from excessive changes in temperature; plants on window sills should be positioned so that curtains, when drawn, can come between them and the glass surface of the window.

Growing in Sunrooms or on Porches

A sunroom or the sheltered section of a porch or verandah provides an ideal environment for most cacti. In addition to solitary plants in pots, there is often enough room for trays or small benches in which mini-gardens can be established. Hanging baskets planted with epiphytic cacti (*Zygocactus*) can also be displayed with great visual impact.

Wintering cacti in a sunroom or sheltered porch should provide no problems for even the least experienced grower, providing the plants have had a chance, with increased ventilation and reduced watering, to harden off in autumn.

In regions with severe winter frosts, some additional protection — covering the plants, at night only, with a plastic frame or paper — may be required for outdoor positions. Smaller plants, of course, can simply be brought indoors until the danger of severe frosts is over.

Growing Outdoors

Some of the most prolifically flowering and colourful cacti I have seen were grown in outdoor gardens. The somewhat harsher environment of open-air cultivation is considered, by many growers, to be ideal for the best development of spines, body shape and flowers. This includes the smaller, globular

Flowering cacti in an outdoor garden

types of *Lobivia, Echinopsis, Gymnocalycium, Acanthocalycium* and *Notocactus*, as well as the columnar cereoid types: *Cleistocactus, Cereus, Trichocereus, Helianthocereus* and *Oreocereus*. The softer-bodied, small cacti — *Mammillaria, Rebutia, Astrophytum, Coryphantha, Neochilenia* and *Parodia* — can also be successfully grown outdoors, providing some form of additional protection from frost and rain is available. Polythene frames or similar semi-permanent structures can provide the required protection.

Good conditions for the establishment and care of outdoor cacti include the following:

1. A well-drained soil profile (a depth of 50–75 centimetres), with a suitable base that enables water to drain away from the roots of the plants. Natural drainage in many gardens can be improved by raising the soil bed in which the cacti have been planted above the surrounding general level of the garden. A supporting wall of bricks or timber can be used for this purpose. In addition, a layer of coarse gravel placed around the base of the plants could provide a further means of draining surplus water away from the roots.

2. The use of average garden soil, provided that it is supplemented by sand, peat and gravel to provide a medium coarse soil mix. Inorganic fertilisers can be added to the soil before planting, at a rate of one handful per square metre.

3. A sheet of polythene stretched over the soil before planting to prevent weed growth among the plants during the years to come. Cacti can then be planted through holes in the polythene and the area between the plants covered with a layer of coarse gravel.

4. Tall, cereoid cacti should be placed towards the back of the garden, with stakes or similar supports to provide protection from wind damage. Large stones or driftwood can be placed among the plants to give the garden a natural appearance.

5. Separate parts of the garden raised to differing levels — with the aid of bricks or a stone wall — can highlight individual groups of cacti and can add greater visual appeal to the whole area.

6. Some protection from frosts or direct rain in more exposed locations. Existing structures, walls or fences can be utilised, as well as the temporary use, in winter, of polythene frames or mulching materials, such as straw.

7. Watering should be limited to periods of prolonged dry weather during the summer months when cacti benefit from additional moisture during active growth and flowering. Take care to avoid splashing the plants with water, as this could lead to rotting and the subsequent loss of plants.

Growing in Frames or Glasshouses

Many of the larger cactus collections are housed under the permanent protection of polythene or glass frames, or in glasshouses. Although expensive, these strucures provide controlled growing conditions in areas where climatic conditions vary considerably between summer and winter. The controlled conditions of a frame or glasshouse also make it possible to raise cactus plants from seed or to grow sensitive types such as *Melocactus* and others that could not be grown outdoors. Generally, plants are grown in pots arranged on shelves or tables. Some growers prefer to raise plants in groups, planting them directly in raised benches or in the soil on the glasshouse floor.

The tall, columnar cacti are usually planted in the centre, or underneath the highest section of a glasshouse or frame, where they can reach their maximum possible size. The

Outdoor collection of G. Barker, Christchurch, New Zealand

smaller, globular cacti are then placed on benches along the structure's sides, so they receive ample light and direct sun. A small area of the glasshouse or frame is also reserved for storage, for repotting and for young plants raised from seed.

Spare headroom can be utilised by planting cacti in hanging baskets.

Major requirements for the successful culture of cacti in covered frames and glasshouses include the following:

1. The avoidance of over-heating and damage from sunburn by the use of ventilation and shading. A simple form of shading can be achieved by spraying the outside of the structure with a lime-water solution. This can be renewed each spring, or as required. Shading cloths, attached to the inside of the strucutre, provide a more permanent protection and these can be removed in winter to increase the amount of light available to the plants. Ventilators can often be left open throughout the summer, except for cold or windy days. Ventilators should be used during fine days, even in winter, to prevent an accumulation of stale air, which would favour the spread of insects and of mould diseases.

2. Design of structures — glasshouses, polythene frames — that allows plants to

Dried up remains of a cholla (*Opuntia*) plant in Arizona

be positioned for easy access for watering and inspection. Poorly watered plants, unsprayed or uncared for — or out of reach — are often lost to pests or disease. The atmosphere around cacti, within a toally covered environment, favours the spread of insects and diseases. Plants should be carefully inspected at regular intervals, and this should be combined with an overall spraying programme if plants are to remain healthy and undamaged (see chapter 3 for recommended sprays).

3. Improved insulation. This, or a limited amount of heating, may be required in districts with severe winter frosts. Winter heating should be restricted to frost periods and should be regulated so that temperatures do not fall below 5–10°C. Excessive heat in winter could lead to renewed plant growth which, in turn, would result in greater frost susceptibility and misshapen cactus forms. Winter heating also dries the air around the plants, and misting should be used to prevent excessive shrivelling.

CHAPTER 3

GROWING CACTI

Propagation by Offsets and Stem Segments

A small number of new plants can be raised each year by separating the new offsets and stem segments from older palnts. Many genera of cactus form such offsets, or side shoots, from the base or sides of their body. In others, the mature sections of stem can be separated by a sharp knife and planted in a new pot to strike roots (see figure 13a).

For some cacti, such as *Rebutia* or *Echinopsis*, the cushion of individual heads can be separated and replanted to form new colonies (see figure 13b).

The taller, cereoid cacti of *Cereus, Trichocereus* and similar genera may not readily form new offsets, although they can be forced to do so by the removal of their growing tip or upper section. Offsets will then form rapidly on the remaining 'mother plant' section, and such plants can become a source of new plant

material for years to come. Growers, who have a need for a regular supply of rootstock material for grafting with *Peireskiopsis* or *Trichocereus* types, use this 'mother plant' technique with success (see figure 13c).

It should be remembered that newly separated sections or offsets should be allowed to heal by drying off in the sun before repotting in order to avoid any rotting of the freshly cut surface. Light dusting with sulphur powder or a similar sanitising agent is used to prevent infection by moulds. However, offsets or the cut surface on a rootstock plant intended for grafting should be used fresh and the area of the cut must not be allowed to dry out before the union is made.

Propagation by Seed

The large-scale propagation of cacti by commercial nurseries or larger growers can only be achieved by using seed. Seeds are sold by specialised seed firms (see appendix) or can be gathered from plants in a grower's collection. Although raising plants on a large scale from seed involves time-consuming attention and specialised care in the glasshouse, practically all growers can raise a small number of cacti from seed. The only sure way to succeed is to experiment and to gain practical skills from handling the minute seedlings, and from learning about the conditions required for different cacti.

A little luck, some skill, and plenty of patience will be required and, although such a knack cannot easily be described, the following suggestions may help those who lack practical experience in this field:

1. Use small containers, made of plastic or other non-porous material, which are

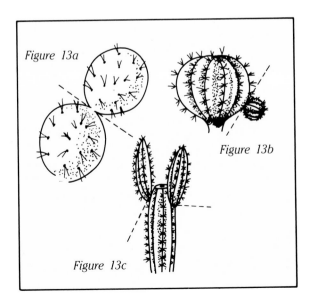

Figure 13a

Figure 13b

Figure 13c

shallow and wide, and which can be covered by glass.

2. To get the best results and strike rate, if you intend growing plants for your own seed, ensure that the seed is freshly gathered. Seeds can be stored in a cool, dry place for many months.

3. Preferably construct a seed box with some bottom heat (as shown in figure 14). Heat is an advantage in the early stages of propagation, as it improves the strike rate and growth of young seedlings. If such a structure cannot be built in time, keep the seedlings in a place that has good light, and ensure that they have even heat and are not exposed to direct sunlight. (More detailed information on making a hot box is included below.)

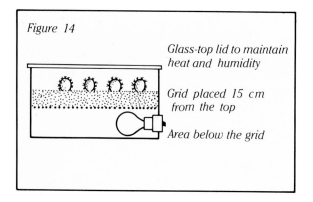

Figure 14

Glass-top lid to maintain heat and humidity

Grid placed 15 cm from the top

Area below the grid

4. The best time for sowing seed is in spring, which will allow the longest possible 'growing on' period before the onset of winter.

5. If glass jars are used as containers for seedlings, they should be deep enough to allow for a base layer of fine gravel or sand (5–7 centimetres), to allow for improved drainage from the soil above. Fill the jars with 'fine mix' soil (see chapter 2), or crushed brick dust, to within 5 centimetres of the top, and compress lightly to provide a level surface for sow-

ing. The soil mix should be sterilised, and this can be done by partly submerging the filled glass jar in boiling water for 50–60 minutes.

6. If plastic containers, such as ice-cream cartons, are used, make pin holes through the bottom of the container to allow for watering and drainage. Before use they should be cleansed by rinsing in hot water and then, when cool, filled with a sterilised soil mix.

7. When the containers are ready for sowing, remove the seeds from the packet and mix them with a small amount of fine sand; this will assist in more even sowing. Spread the seed/sand mixture evenly on the levelled soil and cover with a small amount of additional soil, applied through a fine sieve. Do not bury the seed too deeply. Place the containers in a shallow tray of water and allow them to soak until moisture appears on the surface. Drain away the excess water and place in a 'hot box' structure (figure 14) and cover with glass. In the absence of a hot box, place the container, if possible, in a warm location.

8. Moisten the soil regularly, never allowing it to dry out completely. A gentle misting of the surface is permissible, but bottom soaking is preferable. Make sure you label each container with the relevant name of the parent plant, or from the seed packet. Note the date of sowing and, if applicable, the supplier of the seed.

THE HOT BOX

A hot box can be constructed from wood with a glass top and a grid of metal or wooden laths to hold seed containers. The area below the grid should have an opening to allow for the positioning of an electric light bulb. The size of the box should be related to the bulb size and following proportions are suitable:
⅓ cubic metre (1 cubic foot) — 15 watt bulb;

½ cubic metre (2 cubic feet) — 25 watt bulb; 1 cubic metre (3 cubic feet) — 40 watt bulb. If these proportions are adhered to, the temperature within the seedling box will remain constant at 22–25° Celsius (70–80° Fahrenheit).

Watering by bottom-soaking the seedling containers is done outside an electrically heated box so as to avoid any danger of water coming into contact with the bulb socket or exposed flex. The temperature inside the box should be regularly checked — a thermometer should be placed inside the box for this purpose — to avoid any damage to seeds from overheating. The required amount of heat can be regulated by ventilation or, during hot periods, by switching off the power.

Depending on conditions and the type of cacti, seeds should germinate over a three to ten week period. Not all seeds will germinate at once, so do not be overly concerned at the initially small numbers of plants during the early period after sowing.

Ten to thirteen weeks after sowing, increase the ventilation for young seedlings by slightly raising the glass cover and allowing them to be 'aired' for two to three hours a day. After eighteen weeks, to assist air circulation around the young plants, the glass cover can remain partially open for much of the warm part of the day. Watering, as required, can be correspondingly increased. Maintain a regular pattern of misting and bottom soaking to ensure adequate soil moisture.

TRANSPLANTING SEEDLINGS

Young cactus seedlings can be grafted or transplanted at an early age, usually as soon as the first spines have developed. This stage generally occurs towards the end of summer, and at this stage growers with heated glasshouses transfer their seedlings into open trays.

Unless serious over-crowding occurs, I prefer to keep seedlings in their original containers over winter. In this way the transplanting

Group of ferocacti on a glasshouse bench

and grafting can be done in early spring, and a higher survival rate results. However, when transplanting must be done before winter, it should be completed well before the cold weather starts, to allow the seedlings to become established in their new positions.

The procedures for wintering young seedlings will, in some degree, be similar to those for older plants. Special considerations include:

1. Increased ventilation for the hardening-off period at the end of summer and a reduction of watering. But remember that small seedlings have minimal energy reserves and too harsh conditions of wintering may result in plant loss.

2. Transferring seedling containers indoors, to give them a position of good light and even temperature, is sometimes advisable. Winter temperatures should never be allowed to drop below 10° Celsius, and the soil must be kept slightly moist at all times.

3. Larger, incubator-type boxes, heated by an electric bulb or some similar energy source, can also be used for wintering plants.

4. Misting young seedlings during fine weather is recommended.

5. Limited winter growth of young plants is possible in large nurseries that have heated glasshouses. Ample light with regulated, even heating and a controlled amount of watering will be required.

Transplanting cactus seedlings into open trays involves lifting the minute plants gently from the seedling container and transferring them into prepared trays with a minimum of disturbance to the roots. A special tool can be simply fashioned from a pencil-thick piece of wooden stick, split at one end like a fork, to facilitate, without direct handling, the lifting of seedlings (figure 15).

Glasshouse collection of R. Arnold, Christchurch, New Zealand

Figure 15

Trays for the young plants are usually of wood or plastic, filled with a 'fine soil' mix enriched with a small amount of inorganic fertiliser. A layer of gravel at the base (3 centimetres) will assist in draining any excess water.

Individual plants, or clumps of plants, are placed in rows 2–3 centimetres apart and are grown-on until they reach the required potting or grafting size.

To prevent damage to young plants from sunburn, they should be shaded and kept away from direct sunlight during the hottest part of the day. At a later stage, having benefited from hardening induced by increased ventilation and exposure to light, young plants can be placed in positions similar to those occupied by older plants.

Watering trays by bottom soaking is preferable to direct watering from a tap. Care should be taken not to wet the body of the plant on cold days, or just before nightfall. Misting during hot periods is beneficial as it prevents plants shrivelling and excessive drying of the soil. Adding Chinosol — or a similar fungicide — to the water used for misting will help prevent mould infection in young plants and seedlings. Alkaline, tap water should never be used for watering or misting.

The wintering of one- to two-year-old cacti will prove easier for the second time around.

Only limited misting during fine days will be required to avoid plants shrivelling.

Some of the more sensitive, soft-body cacti will require the more 'even' temperature of an indoor environment, or may require a limited amount of heating in a glasshouse. The more hardy types, reaching 1–2 centimetres in diameter or more, will not have to be watered at all until the following spring.

The potting of young cacti will follow a similar pattern to the repotting of older plants. Soil should be of a medium coarse type and watering should be started as soon as visible growth begins. It is important not to use excessively large containers for small plants. The repotting of rapidly growing young cacti, up to twice a year, is preferable to the use of large pots.

Grafting Cacti

'To graft or not to graft' is often a hotly disputed subject among many growers. In some cases, grafting is necessary to preserve a rare or old plant which, otherwise, would not survive. The new chlorophyll-free plants from Japan — 'yellow peanut cactus' or 'red ball' *Gymnocalycium* and similar mutants — must be grafted in order to grow at all.

Grafting is also considered essential to maintain and develop the appeal of 'cristata' or 'crest' forms of all cacti that grow in a deformed, 'comb-like' fashion. The grafting of mother plants on strongly growing rootstock also allows for more rapid propagation and the growth of many rare and difficult-to-grow cacti — also old plants which have lost roots, new finds from South America, or some soft-bodied cacti such as *Mammillaria* and *Rebutia*.

The slower-growing cacti, or even seedlings, are grafted to speed up their development and bring them sooner to maturity and flowering stage. Some 'epiphytic' tree-growing cacti are also grafted to produce the popular 'standards', such as *Zygocactus, Schlumbergera* and similar 'orchid' cacti.

The opponents of widespread grafting, especially on very tall stocks, argue against the rather unnatural appearance of grafted cacti, especially their blown-up growth pattern which distorts their true shape and flowering. Opponents also claim that some nurseries use stocks that enhance early growth without regard to the longer-term suitability of the match between the stock and the scion.

Much work, however, remains to be done in the area of the selection and breeding of suitable rootstocks that will be compatible with most cactus types. The ideal stock will resemble the scion's growth pattern, will produce a limited number of offshoots from its base and, most of all, will not 'lignify' or harden excessively with age.

The development of dwarfing stocks of lesser vigour will also benefit the growers of smaller, globular cacti by ensuring that the shape of the plants does not become distorted by excess stock vigour. Some 'cristata' forms of soft-bodied cacti, such as *Echinocereus*, can also suffer from over-vigorous rootstock, and subsequent splitting often occurs.

The matching of a plant's vigour with its dormancy requirements and flowering period, and similar aspects, should always be considered before selecting a rootstock:

1. The smaller, globular cacti should preferably be low grafted to maintain their natural appearance.

2. The less vigorous rootstock of the *Trichocereus* type (*spachianus*), which is easy to handle, is suitable for young cacti, though the related *T. pachanoi*, as it does not harden (lignify) excessively below older plants, is often preferred as the more permanent stock.

3. *Trichocereus schickendantsii* is often suitable for the regrafting or the rejuvenation

of older plants: its more succulent growth increases the likelihood of successful grafting.

4. Both *Cereus* and *Echinopsis* have been used in the past for rootstocks, though the vigour and hardening of the former, and the formation of numerous offshoots on the latter, can cause problems.

5. *Peireskiopsis* is the most preferred rootstock for minute seedlings. Its great affinity to most genera of cacti, and the rapid growth and size increase of seedlings are reasons for its popularity. It is easy to handle and to propagate, and most of the professional nurseries use it to bring forward plant maturity. Fully grown plants are then regrafted or rooted into pots for resale.

6. Species of *Selenicereus* and *Harrisia* (*grandiflorus* and *martinii* respectively), are used for the grafting of epiphytic cacti like *Schlumbergera* to form standards.

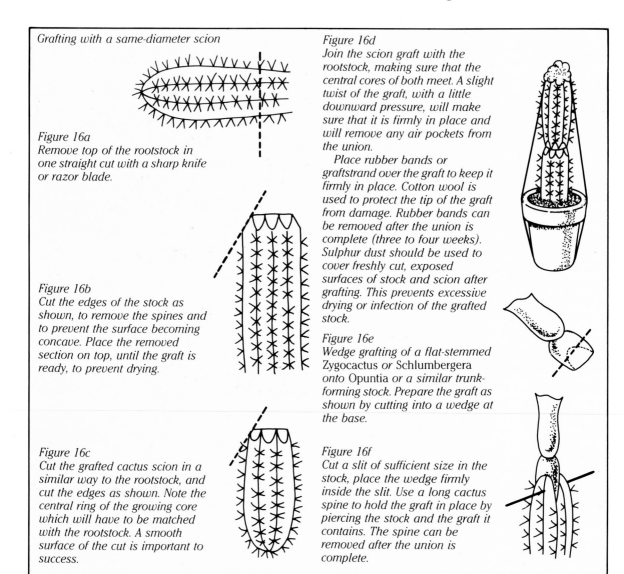

Grafting with a same-diameter scion

Figure 16a
Remove top of the rootstock in one straight cut with a sharp knife or razor blade.

Figure 16b
Cut the edges of the stock as shown, to remove the spines and to prevent the surface becoming concave. Place the removed section on top, until the graft is ready, to prevent drying.

Figure 16c
Cut the grafted cactus scion in a similar way to the rootstock, and cut the edges as shown. Note the central ring of the growing core which will have to be matched with the rootstock. A smooth surface of the cut is important to success.

Figure 16d
Join the scion graft with the rootstock, making sure that the central cores of both meet. A slight twist of the graft, with a little downward pressure, will make sure that it is firmly in place and will remove any air pockets from the union.

Place rubber bands or graftstrand over the graft to keep it firmly in place. Cotton wool is used to protect the tip of the graft from damage. Rubber bands can be removed after the union is complete (three to four weeks). Sulphur dust should be used to cover freshly cut, exposed surfaces of stock and scion after grafting. This prevents excessive drying or infection of the grafted stock.

Figure 16e
Wedge grafting of a flat-stemmed Zygocactus or Schlumbergera onto Opuntia or a similar trunk-forming stock. Prepare the graft as shown by cutting into a wedge at the base.

Figure 16f
Cut a slit of sufficient size in the stock, place the wedge firmly inside the slit. Use a long cactus spine to hold the graft in place by piercing the stock and the graft it contains. The spine can be removed after the union is complete.

7. *Opuntia* and similar segmented stocks have also been used with some success for this purpose.

8. Excellent reports of seedlings grafting on *Hylocereus guatemalensis* are also known (F. Hirata, *Gardeners Chronicle*, 1966), and it is recommended.

In summary, it seems clear that successful grafting will be achieved by growers who select their stock to suit both scion requirements and cultivation conditions. The rootstocks used should be in active growth — as should the scion — during the grafting period of early spring or summer. Techniques of grafting should be practised and all growers, especially the larger nurseries, should carry adequate stocks of grafting material to ensure a steady supply of rootstock at the right time.

Grafting will obviously remain an important technique for the preservation of rare species, for the growing of 'cristata' forms and for the chlorophyll-free cactus mutations. It is likely that grafting will also remain useful as an adjunct to the raising of seedlings.

It is to be hoped that widespread grafting will not be carried out as a general practice with dissimilar genera, as it is desirable that the natural appearance, growth and flowering patterns of these magnificent plants should be able to be observed in future collections.

Finally, despite the complicated appearance of the operation, cacti can be simply and successfully grafted provided that some basic rules are observed (see figures 16 and 17).

Preventing Damage from Splitting and other Growth Deformations

Aside from poor cultivation practices, few, if any, serious problems are likely to confront less experienced growers. The most common problems and their solutions are these:

1. The splitting of cacti after excessive or irregular watering can be avoided by frequent, but not overly generous, watering in spring and summer. Similarly, the

---

Grafting seedlings onto stock with a large diameter

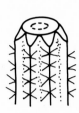

Figure 17a
Prepare the stock in the same way as for grafting with the same-diameter scion as shown in the preceding diagram. Make sure that the stock does not dry out by placing the removed section on top until the graft is ready. The stock should be growing actively during the grafting season.

Figure 17b
Remove the upper two-thirds of the seedling with a sharp knife. Make sure that the cut is level and smooth. Do not cut the edges.

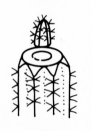

Figure 17c
Place the fresh scion section onto the rootstock in such a way that both central core rings meet. This is achieved by placing the scion directly across the central core-line of the stock. To prevent damage, handle the scion with maximum care.

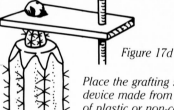

Figure 17d

Grafting spring

Place the grafting spring, or a device made from a narrow strip of plastic or non-corrosive metal, over the graft as shown. An anchoring stick is placed in the soil beside the plant. A small pebble can be used to hold the scion firmly in place, although it is advisable to make sure the weight is not too excessive as this could crush the soft tissues of the seedling being grafted (in many instances the weight of the strip will be sufficient). Avoid disturbing the scion for two to three weeks until the union is complete. Allow for growth of the seedling by removing the strip after this period. Dusting with sulphur is recommended.

Sunset in the Sonora Desert in Arizona

unhealthy and deforming winter growth of plants can be prevented by good exposure to light, cool temperatures, and by reduced watering during the rest period.

2. The excessive drying out of plants is prevented by misting during fine days.

3. Fertilisers, especially those that are nitrogen-rich, should always be used with caution. Splitting and anomalous growth will result from excessive nitrogen.

4. Minor nutrient deficiencies, of boron, for example, can occur in the well-drained, coarse soils used for cacti. Frequent repotting at yearly intervals, or the addition of a balanced nutrient mix with spring watering usually avoids these problems.

5. Older plants, large plants, or those that are sensitive to repotting (*Melocactus* and

others) should be top dressed with a well composted leaf mulch to prevent nutrient deficiency.

Brown Scarring

This is usually caused by exposing plants to excessive heat or strong sunlight. Damage can be avoided by ventilation and by the correct placing of young and more sensitive plants in shaded positions. Brown scarring, or 'mottling', can also be caused by red spider mites (described below).

Ringed Growth Deformations

These are caused by erratic watering, which usually results in a stop-and-start growth pattern. The effects are mostly seen on cereoid or columnar cacti; such damage is prevented by regular watering during the growth period. Damaged plants can be restored by separating the more uniform, younger section near the top and by repotting this top portion and using the base of the cactus as a 'mother plant' for new offshoots.

Rotting and Collapse of Older Plants

When cacti lose roots, or are watered before their active and visible growth begins, the rotting of soft tissues within the plant causes collapse and eventually loss of the complete plant. Letting the soil around the roots and base of the plants stay wet during cold periods also results in rotting.

Rotting can be stopped at an early stage by removing all the infected parts of the roots, or the plant body, with a sharp knife, and by regrafting or rerooting the healthy section.

The yellow or reddish brown coloured tissue is affected first by the rot at the plant centre or core, through which the main feeding veins extend. The discoloured section should be excised down to a colourless or whitish tissue.

Excessive watering of plants in winter, or splashing them with water in summer, should be avoided.

Common Inspect Pests

RED SPIDER MITE (*Tetranychus urticea*)
A yellow-brown mottling of cactus tissue, especially near the growing tip, often indicates damage caused by this sucking insect, a member of the mite family. On closer inspection the mites can be seen by the naked eye to be swarming in profusion, hundreds at a time, all over the plant.

Despite the common name, red spider mite, much of the population observed will be of a yellow-green colour. Their red colouring becomes apparent when, as a result of excessive numbers and lack of food, the mature mites are faced with starvation. However, by then it is usually too late to prevent scarring and damage to plants.

Under conditions less favourable to the mites, their natural predators — other mites and ladybirds — control the population growth without any necessary assistance from the grower.

The hot and dry conditions found in many poorly ventilated glasshouses, or along window sills, favour a rapid multiplication of mites, and as many as ten generations of adult mites will mature in a single summer.

Regular misting of plants during hot weather, combined with ventilation and the use of insecticides, will prevent mites from damaging cacti in glasshouses and other enclosed situations. The use of organo-phosphate-based insecticides (Malathion, Maldison, Dicofol) controls mites satisfactorily, but these insecticides also eliminate the population of predator-mites, so spraying must be repeated at regular intervals.

Spraying is best done during the cooler part of the day, at two-week intervals, or as suggested by the manufacturer. As many of these systemic insecticides are poisonous to humans as well, all sprays must be kept in a safe place. Spraying outdoors should be done in calm conditions with little or no wind; the sprayer, if possible, staying up-wind of the spray. If spraying is to be carried out indoors, the spray must be kept well away from food. All the safety precautions indicated on the label should be strictly adhered to.

The female of the red spider mite over-winters in any suitable and convenient section of the plant — the container or the glasshouse — so it is advisable to fumigate or spray all enclosed growing areas at least once in the spring, or at any time a serious infestation occurs.

Insecticides for controlling sucking insects like mites are also available in powdered form, and these may be safer to use in some situations; it may also be easier to dust the plants than to spray. Dusting should be carried out shortly after misting, as the dust will settle more satisfactorily and result in a better coating of the plants. Cacti grown outdoors are less prone to suffer from mites, although a regular inspection of young growth and of the inaccessible sides of plants may reveal the need for occasional spraying.

MEALY BUG (*Pseudococcus maritimus* and *P. citri*)

Another sucking insect that can cause serious damage is the mealy bug. Mealy bug infestation is easily recognised by whitish spots and a wax-like coating of wool under which the female of the species secretes herself to lay eggs. The sticky substance often hides many colonies of this insect. Dry, sheltered sides of the plant, generally between the ribs, are the most susceptible areas for initial infestation.

A number of generations of mealy bug can mature during a single season; a six to seven

Figure 18a
Adult red spider mite — under 1 millimetre in size — straw-coloured and turning red when faced with starvation.

Figure 18b
Adult white fly — reaches 3 millimetres in size. Damage to plants results from its oval-shaped larvae.

Figure 18c
Adult aphid — approximately 3 millimetres in size. Damages plants by puncturing flower buds and young tissues near the growing tips with its pointed 'beak'.

Figure 18d
Adult, female mealy bug — approximately 1 millimetre in size — without the antennae and wings of the male. Colonies of these insects protect themselves with a cotton-wool-like coverage, which is excreted by the female.

week period produces a mature, female population — larger, pinkish red, and wingless — capable of laying eggs which, once hatched, permit young insects to spread over the other parts of the plant to form new colonies.

Systemic insecticides (such as Malathion and Dimethoate) are used with success to control the mealy bug.

A minor infestation can be simply destroyed by wiping the affected areas of the plant with cotton wool dipped in methylated spirits. It is important to treat all new additions to a collection — especially older plants — against mealy bugs to prevent new infestations.

The 'root' mealy bug (*Rhizoecus falcifer*), which lives off cactus roots deep in the soil, can be more difficult to detect. By the time the grower discovers the infestation it may be too

Encephalocarpus strobiliformis

Echinopsis aureus

precaution, all plants and their root systems should be inspected if they show, without an obvious reason, signs of poor growth or appear to suffer from loss of roots.

Excellent remedies are available to combat white flies and aphids, which can also cause damage, and regular spraying with systemic insecticides is recommended.

See figures 18a–d for identification.

Mould Infections

The 'damping off' or collapse of young seedlings can be caused by a rapid growth of mould. Much seedling loss can be attributed to rapid increases in alkalinity (high pH value) in seedling boxes. By bottom soaking, the salinity of the upper soil layer increases to a level where most seedlings loose their roots and become infected by mould. The use of a low-pH value 'peat' mix (see fine soil mixes, chapter 2) or crushed brick (finely sieved) prevents much of this problem. The use of fungicide (such as Benlate, Chinosol, Captan) in watering will prevent the growth of mould.

Mould infections of freshly cut or damaged tissue, which may occur in repotting or with offset separations, can be prevented by adequate, wound healing ('callusing'). Callusing can be achieved by the exposure of cut surfaces, such as stem or roots, to warm and dry air for a period of seven to ten days. The use of sulphur dust to prevent mould infection is recommended.

Rapid root system development can be achieved by placing the healed (callused) portion of the plant base near a water surface (see figure 19). This technique may be vital for the preservation of old or imported plants that have lost their roots in transit and appear to have a well lignified (hardened) base.

Any planting of insufficiently healed plants, or root, will result in infection and in subsequent plant rot. To combat mould it is important to use sulphur dust to prevent infection.

late, and a large part of the roots, or the whole plant, can be lost. Regular, yearly repotting assists in early detection of root mealy bug and identifies plants that are in danger. Flooding the soil with systemic insecticides, and the addition of paradichlorobenzene crystals in the potting mix, are an essential part of preventive action against this parasite. As a

---

Figure 19

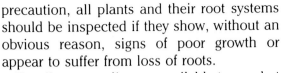

Jar almost filled with water and containing a globular cactus held about 5 centimetres above the liquid

CHAPTER 4

ILLUSTRATED GUIDE
TO CACTUS GENERA
AND SPECIES

Echinopsis mamilosa var. *kermesina*

Echinopsis	*ancistrophora* forma *cristata* *coronata* *haku-jomaru* *mamilosa* var. *kermesina* *multiplex* *obrepanda* var. *purpurosea* *rhodotricha* hybrid: 'red pygmy' hybrid: 'stars and stripes' hybrid: 'sunset' Paramount hybrid group	100	*Harrisia*	*tortuosa*	133
			Helianthocereus	*huascha*	134
			Hertrichocereus	*beneckei*	135
			Homalocephala	*texensis*	136
			Horridocactus	*paucicostatus FR 493* *robustus* var. *vagasanus* sp. nov. (Ritter)	137
Encephalocarpus	*strobiliformis*	104	*Islaya*	*grandiflorens* *maritima* *unguispina*	139
Epiphyllopsis	*gaertnerii*	105			
Epiphyllum	*ackermannii* *grandilobum*	106	*Lepismium*	*cruciforme*	140
			Leuchtenbergia	*principis*	141
Epithelantha	*micromeris* *micromeris* var. *tuberosa*	107	*Lobivia*	*backebergii* *calineana* *densispina* *densispina* var. *blossfeldii*	142
Erdisia	sp. nov. (Menrath)	108			
Eriocactus	*leninghausii* *leninghausii* var. *cristata* *magnificus* *schumannianus*	109			
Eriocereus	*justbertii, tephracanthus*	111			
Escobaria	*alamoensis* *chaffeyii* *gigantea* *runyonii*	112			
Espostoa	*lanata* *mirabilis FR 670* *ritterii* forma *cristata*	114			
Eulychnia	*ritterii*	117			
Ferocactus	*acanthodes* *coloratus* *echidne* *fordii* *mostii* var. *kurtzianum* *quehlianum* var. *zantnerianum* *saglione* var. *tilcarensis* *valnicekianum*	118			
Gymnocereus	*microspermus*	130			
Haageocereus	*decumbens* *multangularis*	131			
Hamatocactus	*chihuahuaensis* *hamatacanthus* *setispinus*	132			

Gymnocalycium gibbosum var. *negrum*

Parodia (contd)	*maasii* var. *carminatiflora FR 46c* (Ritter)	
	maasi var. *rubrispina* forma *cristata*	
	maasii var. *suprema*	
	obtusa FR 1125 (Ritter)	
	ocampoi FR 738 (Ritter)	
	subterranea FR 731 (Ritter)	
	suprema FR 912 (Ritter)	
	tredecimcostata FR 739 (Ritter)	
	tilcarensis	
	yamparaezii	

Pediocactus	*peeblesianus*	187
	simpsonii	

Pelecyphora	*aselliformis*	188

Pereskia	*aculeata*	189

Pfeiffera	*mataralensis FR 363*	190

Pilosocereus	*floccosus*	191
	palmerii	

Pseudolobivia	*aurea*	192

Pterocactus	*fischeri*	193
	tuberosus	

Rebutia	*glomeriseta*	194
	grandiflora	
	krainziana	
	marsonerii	
	senilis var. *iseliniana*	
	vallegrandensis	

Rhipsalidopsis	*gaertnerii*	196
	rosea	

Rhipsalis	hybrid 'China Rose'	197
	sp.	

Rooksbya	*euphorbioides*	198

Roseocactus	*fissuratus*	199
	fissuratus var. *lloydii*	
	kotschoubeyanus	

Selenicereus	*grandiflorus*	200

Seticereus	*icosagonus*	201

Setiechinopsis	*mirabilis*	202

Soehrensia	*bruchii*	203
	formosa	
	ingens	
	quebrada	

Solisia	*pectinata*	205

Neoporteria litoralis

Strombocactus	*disciformis*	206

Sulcorebutia	*hoffmanniana*	207
	mentosa FR 945 (Ritter)	
	menesesii	
	steinbachii	
	totorensis	
	tunariensis	
	weingartiana	

Tephrocactus	*aoracanthus* (= *T. articulatus* var. *ovatus*)	208
	articulatus var. *papyracanthus*	
	ovatus	
	rosea	

Thelocactus	*bicolor*	212
	bueckii	
	heterochromus	
	leucacanthus var. *schmollii*	
	nidulans	
	wagnerianus	

ACANTHOCALYCIUM Backeberg

HABITAT
Small to medium-sized, globular cacti from northern Argentina.

These are hardy plants with a preference for sunny positions, coarse soil mixes and winter rest. They can be grown well on their own roots or may be grafted.

BODY
Small to medium in size, spherical, but becomes slightly elongated with age. Clearly defined ribs, green to blue-grey in colour.

SPINES
Usually thin and bristly, but they can also be short and thick. Centrals are scarcely distinguishable, and are sometimes darker tipped. The colour of spines varies from straw yellow to dark brown.

FLOWERS
Blooms from mid to late summer; the flowers are large, attractive and funnelform in shape. Colours can be white, pale green-yellow, rich yellow or delicate shades of mauve and red.

A noticeable ring of wool at the base of the flower tube and the spiny scales of the flower buds are typical. Flowers rise from the crown or upper part of the body.

PROPAGATION
Most species do not offset freely unless they are grafted. Many growers propagate from seeds with little difficulty.

A. glaucum FR 970

SPECIES
From the dozen or so species of *Acanthocalycium* that have been classified, the following are those seen most often in cultivation: *A. aurantiacum*, *A. glaucum*, *A. griseum*, *A. klimpelianum*, *A. peitscherianum*, *A. spiniflorum* and *A. violaceum*.

A. klimpelianum

A. violaceum

A. peitscherianum

A. spiniflorum

ACANTHOLOBIVIA Backeberg

Subgenus of *Lobivia* according to W. Rausch

HABITAT
Small, spherical cacti, closely related to genus *Lobivia*, from the highlands of Peru. Distinctive spiny fruits and night flowering differentiate this genus from *Lobivia*.

Hardy cactus with a preference for a sunny position, coarse soil mix, and dry, winter rest. Grows well on its own roots.

BODY
A small, sometimes offsetting, spherical body. Green in colour.

SPINES
Spines are usually horn coloured and curved. The central spine is hardly distinguishable.

FLOWERS
Lobivia-like, bell-shaped flowers are about approximately 5 centimetres long. They arise from the lower part of the body in mid-summer. Sulphur yellow to red in colour and self-fertile. The fruit is green and has spination.

PROPAGATION
From offsets or seed.

SPECIES
The two named species are *A. incuiensis* and *A. tegeleriana*.

Acantholobivia tegeleriana

ANCISTROCACTUS Britton & Rose

Subgenus of *Echinocactus* according to L. Benson

HABITAT
Small to medium-sized cacti with distinctively attractive spination and prolific flowers, from the southern states of the United States and Mexico.

Large tap root and hooked central spine typical. Coarse soil mix, sunny position and dry wintering are important. Often grafted as older plants on their own roots, these cacti can be difficult to maintain.

BODY
Although spherical at first, the older plants elongate; there is a noticeable restriction at the plant's base and a thickened tap root. These cacti are tuberculate, have well-defined ribs, and are dark green to greyish green in colour.

FLOWERS
Arising from areoles near the top, the flowers are numerous with typically scaly buds. Flowers are small in size, yellow, cream or pink in colour, formed during early to mid-summer. Flowering can be expected with young plants.

PROPAGATION
Does not offset, so seed propagation is usually employed.

SPECIES
From the few species classified, the following are better known: *A. brevihamatus* and *A. scheeri.*

A. scheerii

APOROCACTUS Lemaire

HABITAT
An attractive epiphytic plant from Mexico.
   Ideally suited to hanging baskets, or it will
require support for its creeping, thin branches.
Grows well on its roots in coarse, well-drained
soil, in diffused light rather than full sun. Dry
winter rest and a position with ample fresh air in
summer will result in profuse flowering.
Development of aerial roots and susceptibility to
red spider mite are typical.

BODY
Thin, long and creeping or pendant branches,
large aerial roots. Green to grey-green in colour.
Thin ribs. Branching freely. Spination is short,
usually reddish brown in colour.

FLOWERS
Aporocactus flowers profusely from the sides of
the stems exposed to light. The flower is
zygomorphic, medium-sized and bright in colour,
deep crimson red or pink, in mid-summer.

PROPAGATION
Relatively easy to propagate by cuttings or by
separation of individual branches; rarely grown
from seed.

SPECIES
The two best-known species in collections are
A. flagelliformis and *A. martianus*.

A. flagelliformis

AREQUIPA Britton & Rose

HABITAT
Native to Peru and northern Chile, *Arequipa* plants are not difficult to maintain, and they will flower given coarse soil mix, position of full sun and dry winter rest. Short cereoid to prostrate-growing cacti with slender branches and attractive flowers.

BODY
Spherical at first, in maturity the body is short, cereoid, with branches often forming low groups. Semi-upright to prostrate in growth. Thin ribs and crowded areoles are typical. Spines are thin, radials are needle-like and centrals stouter.

FLOWERS
Zygomorphic flowers have a long flower tube and are attractively coloured from carmine to deep red, up to 8 centimetres long. They appear in late summer.

PROPAGATION
By separating branches or usually by seed.

SPECIES
The following are often seen in collections: *A. hempeliana*, *A. leucotricha*, *A. mirabilis* and *A. rettigii*.

A. mirabilis (juvenile form)

A. rettigii

A. leucotricha

A. hempeliana

ARIOCARPUS Scheidwer

HABITAT
One of the more difficult of Mexican cacti, *Ariocarpus* is closely related to *Roseocactus*, which it resembles in all but some details.

These are slow-growing plants unless grafted. Typically in nature, the plant is almost buried in soil and difficult to find. It prefers a coarse soil mix with a high stone content and minimal watering. Dry winter rest is essential. Greatly thickened tap root is typical.

BODY
Broadly rounded, slow-growing plants with ribs formed by elongated tubercles arranged in a spiral. Greyish green in colour. The body is crowned with wool, from which the flowers arise.

FLOWERS
Pale pink, yellow or white in colour, flowers appear in mid to late summer. It flowers apically from tufts of wool, the flowers being arranged in a circle around the apex, sometimes with several flowers from one axil. Flowering occurs in mature plants.

SPECIES
Species seen in collections are *A. elongatus*, *A. furfuraceus*, *A. retusus* and *A. trigonus*.

A. trigonus var. *elongatus*

A. trigonus

A. retusus (juvenile form)

A. furfuraceus

ARROJADOA Britton & Rose

HABITAT
Thin-branched, cereoid cacti from northern Brazil.

Although not commonly seen in collections, species of *Arrojadoa* are attractive and unusual in appearance. The plant's apex is covered by bristly tufts of modified spines, from which the flowers arise. Night flowering and spherical fruits are typical. These cacti are usually grafted, as they are rather slow-growing on their own roots. A coarse soil mix, position of diffused light, and winter rest are recommended.

BODY
Cereoid, up to 1 metre in length and branching from the base, especially when grafted. It has slender branches with thin ribs and bristly spines of attractive golden to light brown colour. Mature plants usually require support.

FLOWERS
Flowers arise from the apical tuft of bristles and are night-flowering and red in colour. The small flowers are arranged in circle near apex. Plants on their own roots must reach near full-size maturity before flowering occurs; grafted plants flower more freely. Flowers appear in mid to late summer.

PROPAGATION
By offsets or by seed.

SPECIES
Half a dozen species are classified, amongst which the following deserve attention:
A. aureispina, *A. penicillata* and *A. rhodantha*.

A. *rhodantha* (mature plant)

A. *rhodantha* (juvenile form)

ASTROPHYTUM Lemaire

Subgenus of *Echinocactus* according to L. Benson

HABITAT
One of the best-known of all the cactus genera, *Astrophytum* come from Texas and the eastern parts of Mexico.

The familiar bishop's cap cactus (*A. myriostigma*) is completely spineless; other species have long, flexible or rigid spines. Minute, white flakes cover the bodies of some *Astrophytum* plants; in others this is not so obvious.

All *Astrophytum* species prefer a well-drained, coarse soil mix and a dry winter rest. A sunny position induces plentiful flowering with large and attractive blooms. All species grow well on their own roots, although grafting will increase the speed of growth in younger plants and seedlings. They prefer neutral to slightly alkaline soils; soil adjustment is achieved by the adding of small amounts of gypsum. If required, pH levels can be checked using the litmus paper method described in chapter 2.

BODY
Young plants are spherical to slightly elongated and of moderate size. Older plants become elongated with age, and one species (*A. ornatum*) can reach 1 metre in height.

The body colour is green with varying amounts of white flakes, which give some species a characteristic, greyish appearance. The few acute angles in the shape of bishop's cap cactus become clearly defined; other species have narrow ribs.

FLOWERS
Blooms are produced in mid to late summer from the woolly buds on the crown. The large flowers are in various shades of yellow, sometimes with a red centre. The plants must attain a sufficient age and size before flowering — usually after three to five years — although grafted plants will flower sooner.

A. asterias

A. capricorne

A. *myriostigma* var. *nudum*

A. *ornatum* var. *mirbelii*

PROPAGATION

Unless grafted, offshoots are rarely seen and most growers propagate *Astrophytum* from their large seeds.

SPECIES

From the handful classified, the following species are the best known: *A. asterias*, *A. capricorne*, *A. myriostigma*, *A. ornatum* and *A. senile*.

A. *capricorne* var. *major*

AYLOSTERA Spegazzini

Subgenus of *Rebutia* according to E. Götz

HABITAT
A popular, freely offsetting and flowering genus from southern Bolivia and northern Argentina.

In more recent times this genus has been included with the closely related *Rebutia* (Ritter, Buining and others). However, Backeberg's original classification (*Kakteenlexikon*, 1966) separated *Aylostera* from *Rebutia* because of differences in flower structure. In *Aylostera*, the flower tube is always united with the style, giving the slender tube a stem-like appearance.

Aylostera are easy-to-grow plants with strikingly beautiful flowers. The plants prefer a coarse soil mix, full sun and a dry winter rest. They can either be grown on their own roots or grafted.

BODY
Small, spherical and soft-bodied; if offsetting is allowed, the heads will gradually form cushions. The ribs are formed from rows of more or less distinct tubercles, which give these plants their characteristic appearance of perfect symmetry. The body is pale to dark green in colour.

SPINES
Thin, bristly and short; straight or slightly curving. Their colour varies from silvery white to pale or reddish brown.

FLOWERS
Blooms can be expected from early to mid-summer. The slender flower tube rises from the base of the plant and tends to be hairy and bristly.

All species have brightly coloured flowers, mostly flame or carmine red, and even young, two-year-old plants will flower well if cultivated under the right conditions.

PROPAGATION
As this genus produces offsets freely, new plants can be formed readily and simply by breaking up the cushions of individual heads.

In large nurseries, seedlings are grown with little difficulty. Grafting the mother plants considerably speeds up the formation and growth of offsets. *Peireskiopsis* rootstock has been used with success when making grafts.

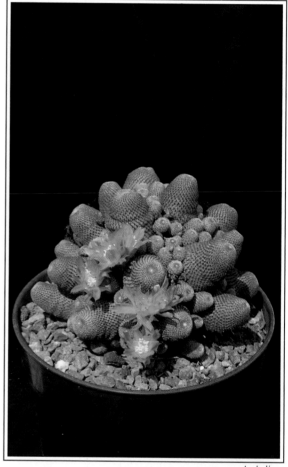

A. heliosa

A. fulviseta

A. muscula FR 753

A. pseudodeminuta

SPECIES

Twenty species are listed by Backeberg; many of these, however, have been classified as *Rebutia* or *Chileorebutia* by Ritter and others. From the species that have been grown in collections the following have shown special merit: *A. albiflora*, *A. albipilosa*, *A. deminuta*, *A. fiebrigii*, *A. fulviseta*, *A. kupperiana*, *A. muscula*, *A. maxima*, *A. pseudodeminuta*, *A. pseudominiscula* and *A. spinossima*.

AYLOSTERA Spegazzini

A. maxima

A. sp. nov. (Menrath)

A. miniscula

A. fiebrigii

A. sp. nov. *FR 756* (Ritter)

AZTEKIUM Bödecker

HABITAT
Low-growing, spherical plants from Mexico, with a typically folded surface of the main ribs.

Attractive for their unusual body form rather than their small, white flowers, *Aztekium* plants are not easy to maintain and are slow growing on their own roots, so many collectors keep these cacti grafted. A coarse soil mix of high mineral content and dry winter rest and careful summer watering are recommended.

BODY
The bodies of these cacti are broadly spherical and slow-growing, and they do not offset until maturity is reached. Thickened roots and a body divided into a series of large ribs that have a typically folded surface are also characteristic. Spination is sparse, short and thin. Grey-green in colour.

FLOWERS
Flowering, which occurs in mid to late summer, requires a full sunny position and maturity. Flowers, small and white, appear from tufts of wool on plant's apex. Fruits are pink.

PROPAGATION
These cacti rarely offset until mature size is reached, so they are usually raised from seed.

SPECIES
One species only has been classified, *A. ritterii*.

A. ritterii

71

AZUREOCEREUS Akers & Johnson

Subgenus of *Browningia* according to E. Götz

HABITAT
Tall, tree-like cerei from highlands in Peru.
  Attractive and hardy plants, these are best
suited to large containers, dry, coarse soil mix
and sparse winter watering. They rarely flower
before reaching several metres in height.

BODY
Tall, up to 10 metres in height, branching above
to form a tree-like shape. Stout, deep ribs and
epidermis frosted-blue in colour.

SPINES
Stout spines with projecting centrals, up to 10
centimetres long and dark tipped. Radiating
spines are yellow-brown to grey colour.

FLOWERS
The large, nocturnal flowers are cylindrical in
shape, and white in colour. A scaly flower tube
typical. Flowers are 5 centimetres in diameter.

PROPAGATION
Usually by seed.

SPECIES
A. hertlingianus is the best-known species.

A. hertlingianus var. *monstrosus*

BARTSCHELLA Britton & Rose

Subgenus of *Mammillaria* according to E. Götz

HABITAT
Small, *Mammillaria*-like cacti from Baja California region of Mexico.

Separated from *Mammillaria* on account of its large flower and lack of milky sap, it is nonetheless listed as a subgenus of *Mammillaria* by most authors. Coarse soil mix, dry winter rest and sunny position suit these cacti well. They can be grown on their own roots or grafted.

BODY
The body is small, but becomes slightly elongated with age, and is green coloured. Tubercles are broadly circular, forming clearly defined ribs. Offsets form from the base. These cacti have attractive spination with central spines hooked and dark tipped.

FLOWERS
Flowers are large — up to 4 centimetres in diameter — and reddish purple in colour; the fruit is bright red. Flowering occurs in early summer.

PROPAGATION
From offsets or by seed.

SPECIES
A single species has been described, *B. schumannii*.

B. schumannii

BLOSSFELDIA Werdermann

Subgenus of *Mammillaria* according to E. Götz

HABITAT
The smallest of all cacti, *Blossfeldia* plants reach
flowering size at about 1 centimetre in diameter.
They are native to Bolivia and Argentina.

All species lack discernible ribs or spination
and offset easily. A coarse soil mix, dry winter
rest, and a position of full sun are recommended.
These cacti are often grafted, though they also
grow well on their own roots. The tap root is
noticeably thickened, and the plants are sensitive
to over-watering.

BODY
A very small body, which forms clumps through
frequent offsets. Greyish green in colour, and
more or less glossy, these cacti have minimal
development of ribs or spines. Spiral arrangement
of areoles. The tap root is typically enlarged.

FLOWERS
Small, usually white to greenish white flowers
appear during early to mid-summer. Flowers arise
from the apex.

PROPAGATION
Usually by offsets or from the glossy, brown seed.

SPECIES
From the handful described, the following are
seen in collections: *B. campaniflora*, *B. liliputana*,
B. minima FR 750, *B. pedicellata FR 749*.

B. liliputana

74

BOLIVICEREUS Cárdenas

Subgenus of *Borzicactus* according to E. Götz

HABITAT
These slender-branched cerei of semi-upright to prostrate form, growing up to 2 metres in height, come from Bolivia and northern Peru.

Attractive cacti, the bright red to flame red flowers arise profusely from the sides of mature branches. These cacti require some form of support when fully grown. Species of *Bolivicereus* grow well on their own roots in a sunny position. Soil of high mineral content and coarse structure is best suited to them. A dry winter rest is essential. The genus *Bolivicereus* is sometimes mentioned in the literature as a subgenus of *Borzicactus* (Kimnach).

BODY
Formed by slender cereoid branches that offset from the base. Reaching a height of up to 2 metres, in a semi-upright form, these cacti have clearly defined ribs and short spination of yellow to brown colour. Central spines in some species are slightly longer than the radials.

FLOWERS
These are freely flowering cacti, with bright red flowers borne on the flanks of mature shoots in mid-summer. The flower tube is long and slender, noticeably oblique and bent, with or without bristly hair development at the base of the flower tube. The fruit is spherical, and fruits are covered with dense brown hair.

PROPAGATION
From offsets, cuttings or the very small seed.

SPECIES
The best-known and most collected species include *B. chacoanus FR 841*, *B. samaipatanus* and *B. tenuiserpens*.

B. samaipatanus

B. bolivicereus × *winteria* (hybrid)

BRASILICACTUS Backeberg

Subgenus of *Notocactus* according to E. Götz

HABITAT
One of the most attractive of all spherical cacti, *Brasilicactus* species are native to the grasslands of northern Argentina and southern Brazil.

Sometimes *Brasilocactus* is referred to genus *Notocactus*, although some flower differences do exist. Popular for their fine spination and bright flowers, all species grow well on their own roots and appear more attractive than the grafted versions. A medium coarse soil mix and sunny position are preferred by these cacti. A dry winter rest is recommended.

BODY
Broadly spherical to rounded, the body has numerous, thin ribs and small, dense areoles. The body is greyish green in colour. These cacti rarely offset if they are not grafted.

SPINES
Spines are thin, long and bristly, attractively coloured, from silvery white to bright golden. Central spines are slightly longer, and sometimes darker, than the radials. There is also noticeable spination on the flower tube and fruits.

FLOWERS
Relatively small flowers appear profusely from the apex in early spring. Just 1 to 2 centimetres long, the flowers are bright red; the fruits are green.

PROPAGATION
Usually from seed.

SPECIES
From the few species described, the following command attention: *B. graessnerii* and *B. haselbergii*.

B. graesnerii

B. haselbergii

CEPHALOCEREUS Pfeiffer

HABITAT
Known best as the old man cactus, *Cephalocereus* is a large, cereoid cactus reaching up to 15 metres in height and rarely branching. The 'old man' appearance is largely due to a covering of long, tangled white hair, all over the cactus, pointing downward. Native to Mexico, these cacti grow well on their own roots in a sunny position in a coarse soil mix with gypsum added for increased alkalinity. These cacti are slow growing, so grafting is often used to increase the size of young plants.

BODY
A stoutly cereoid green body, with clearly formed ribs, is covered in a thick growth of white, bristly hair. In nature, these plants reach over 12 metres in height, but, unless grafted, flowering plants over 1 metre high are rare in collections. Rarely branch from the base.

SPINES
Spines are 3 to 4 centimetres long, greyish white in colour, and appear among the forty or so long hairs arising from each areole.

FLOWERS
Flowering rarely seen in collections, as the plant must reach over 4 metres in height. The flowering zone is true cephalium, starting on one side of the branch near the apex, but later enveloping the whole tip of the shoot. Cephalium is formed by a growth of longer, bristly wool of creamy colour. Flowers are 10 to 12 centimetres long, white with a pink tube, and hairy at the base. Fruits are red with reddish pulp. Flowering occurs in mid to late summer.

PROPAGATION
Usually by seed.

SPECIES
A single species only has been described, *C. senilis*.

C. senilis

CEPHALOCLEISTOCACTUS Ritter

Subgenus of *Cleistocactus* according to E. Götz

HABITAT
A genus of slender-branched columnar cacti from
eastern Bolivia, these cacti are separated from
other cleistocacti on account of the bristly flower
zone (cephalia) near the apex from which the
flowers arise.

Cacti of this genus reach from 1 metre to 5
metres in height. Their branches form colonies,
joined at their base. In collections they grow well
without support and on their own roots. A coarse
soil mix, dry winter rest and a sunny position are
preferred.

BODY
Slender cacti, with tall branches characterised by
numerous narrow ribs and a profusion of bristly,
short spines of creamy white colour. A tuft of
longer spines forms the flowering zone near the
apex. Offsetting from the base. Depending on the
species, these cacti reach a height of 1 to 5
metres.

FLOWERS
Flowers arise from a true cephalium, that is, the
bristly flowering zone on one side or encircling
the apex of a flowering branch. Flowers are more
or less cylindrical, with a narrow tube 4 to 5
centimetres long and slightly bent. Flowers are
yellow or red. Flowering in early to mid-summer.

PROPAGATION
By separating offsets or by seed.

SPECIES
The most popular species in collections include
C. pallidus, *C. ritterii* and *C. schattatianus*.

C. ritterii

CEREUS Miller

HABITAT
The natural distribution of *Cereus* extends from some isolated populations in the West Indies, through the northern parts of South America, to as far as eastern Argentina and Brazil.

One of the earliest known and most widespread members of the cactus family belongs to the large genus called *Cereus*. These tall, columnar cacti grow to tree-size and have stout trunks and a crown of branches with large ribs (1). Some species of *Cereus* appear as smaller shrubs, low-growing and less upright (2), but most will reach several metres in height. Because of their hardy nature and striking appearance, *Cereus* cacti are well suited to outdoor culture or to large glasshouses.

In regions with severe winters, the younger plants will require protection from frosts, but in most gardens healthy specimens can be cultivated in well-drained soils with a sunny and sheltered position near a wall, or some similar shelter from the wind.

Except for the well-known monstrose form of *C. peruvianus*, the plant is usually grown on its own roots.

BODY
Fresh green to bluish green in colour, usually stout, and branching well above ground. The ribs are large and set well apart in exact fashion, giving *Cereus* plants their symmetrical appearance. Lower growing, bushy species also exist.

SPINES
Thick and long, the central spines are often much longer and darker in colour. Usually light to dark brown or almost black, and often darker tipped.

FLOWERS
Flowering often occurs only after mature height has been reached. The nocturnal flowers are 20–30 centimetres long; many are scented, and they vary in colour from pure white to pink and deep red. The flower tube is glabrous, and the fruit is yellowy green or red. Flowering occurs late in summer.

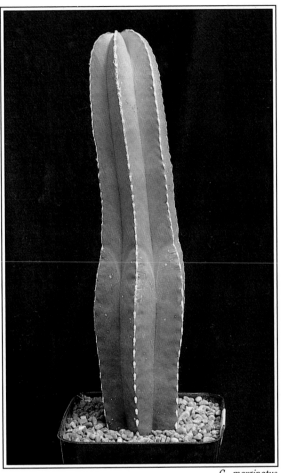

C. marginatus

C. giganteus

CEREUS

C. giganteus forma *cristata*

PROPAGATION
Offsets from older plants and individual branches can be used. Removing the growing tip will increase the number of offsets formed, and this so-called 'mother plant' method of propagation is popular. Seeds are used by large nurseries to raise the fast-growing *Cereus* plants to saleable size in a single season.

SPECIES
From the numerous species found in nature, the following are often seen in collections:
C. aethiops(2), *C. argentinensis(1)*, *C. azureus(1)*, *C. glaucus(1)*, *C. hexagonus(1)*, *C. peruvianus(2)* and its monstrose form, *C. validus(2)*, *C. milesimus(2)*, *C. tacuaralensis(1)* and *C. giganteus(1)*.

C. thurberii

C. peruvianus

CHIAPASIA Britton & Rose

Subgenus of *Discocactus* according to Kimnach

HABITAT
Slender-stemmed epiphytes from Mexico. Humus-enriched soil mix, a position of diffused light and limited watering over winter months suit these plants well.

BODY
Slender, flattened stems with terete trunks. Branching freely. Spines absent.

FLOWERS
Bell-shaped to funnelform, lilac-pink flowers are up to 5 centimetres long. Flowering occurs in mid to late summer.

PROPAGATION
By separating individual stems.

SPECIES
C. nelsonii.

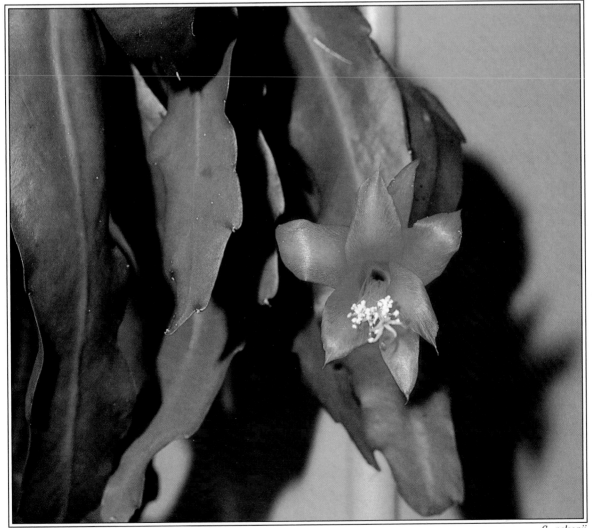

C. nelsonii

CLEISTOCACTUS Lemaire

HABITAT

These plants are found in central Peru, eastern Bolivia, northern Argentina, in Paraguay and in parts of Uruguay.

A large group of low to medium height, cereoid cacti, which form colonies of slender, branched shrubs. Growth is mainly upright, and many species reach 50–150 centimetres in height. A few *Cleistocactus* species grow taller, *C. morawetzianus* reaching several metres in height.

These are attractive plants, admired for their fine spination of dense, bristly spines and for their flame-coloured flowers, which rise in rows from the sides of each mature branch.

Cleistocacti are hardy plants and for that reason easy to grow. A well-drained, coarse soil mix, winter rest without watering, and a sunny position will suit these cacti well. Cleistocacti are grown on their own roots.

BODY

Slender, 2–5 centimetres in diameter, with sometimes more robust stems, ranging from 50 to 150 centimetres in height, which branch from the base to form shrubs. The shallow ribs are numerous, well defined, light to dark green in colour, and sometimes transversely furrowed.

SPINES

Fine, mostly short and bristly, sometimes interspersed with longer and thicker central spines. Colouring varies from pure white, through yellow-cream to brown; centrals are often darker tipped.

FLOWERS

A wide range of colours from white and yellow to flame red. The flowers have a slender cylindrical tube with a narrow opening. Many species are cleistogamic, that is, they produce seed from unopened flowers. The base of the flower tube is always hairy.

A degree of plant maturity has to be reached — which will depend on cultivation conditions, and may take a few years — before flowering takes place. Flowering occurs in early to mid-summer.

C. candelilla

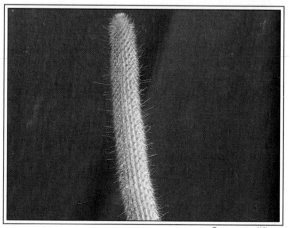

C. smaragdiflorus

C. bayanii

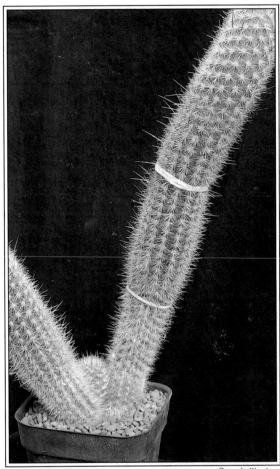

C. subtilispinus

C. hyalacanthus (with seed pod)

PROPAGATION
At home, by separating branches from the base,
or by using the mother plant technique and
repotting the separated top. In nurseries, by seed.

SPECIES
Including some of the more recently named finds
by Ritter, the following are recommended for
cultivation: *C. angosturensis*, *C. ayopayanus*,
C. baumannii, *C. chacoanus*, *C. clavicaulis*,
C. crassicaulis, *C. flavispinus*, *C. hildewinterae*,
C. hyalacanthus, *C. morawetzianus*, *C. parviflorus*,
C. strausii, *C. tarijensis*, *C. vallegrandensis* and
C. viridiflorus.

COCHEMIEA (K. Brandegee) Walton

Subgenus of *Mammillaria* according to E. Götz

HABITAT
Cushion-forming, cylindrical plants from Baja
California in Mexico.

These are attractive cacti, with colourful
spination, hooked central spines and bright red
flowers, although flowering occurs only after the
cactus reaches a reasonably mature size. A
coarse soil mix, dry winter rest and a sunny
position are recommended. These cacti usually
grow well on their own roots.

BODY
Elongated, cylindrical shape, with ribs formed by
rows of tubercles, without milky sap. Dense
colonies are formed by branching at base.
Branches can be up to 30 centimetres tall.

SPINES
Radiating spines are grey to reddish brown, 1
centimetre long and stiff. The central spines are
usually attractively coloured, darker, hooked, and
5 centimetres long.

FLOWERS
The flowers are moderately large, at 5 centimetres
long, bright red in colour, and arising near the
branch tip from axils. Flowering occurs in mid-
summer on mature branches. The fruits are
usually red.

PROPAGATION
By offsets or by seed.

SPECIES
The best-known cultivated species include
C. maritima, *C. poselgerii* and *C. setispina*.

C. setispina

C. poselgerii

COPIAPOA Britton & Rose

HABITAT

All *Copiapoa* plants so far named come from a rather limited geographical area in Chile, and many intermediate forms between the species are known.

This is a genus of spherical cacti, with two principal forms of growth. The first group comprises small cacti, spherical in shape, which, by offsetting, form low cushions of plants (1). The second group contains larger plants, which do not offset easily and become elongated with age (2).

Natural hybridisations among a limited number of ancestral types have possibly resulted in the variations observed in a number of recent finds, and it could be argued, and sometimes is, that many new names are simply forms or variants of previously known species that originated from the northern and central parts of Chile.

Copiapoas are hardy cacti. They are often slow-growing, but the smaller types flower freely at an early age. The taller, columnar species must often reach maturity before flowering occurs. All species are attractive, having a wide variation of colourful spines, body form and colouring.

A well-drained, coarse soil mix with a sunny position and limited watering during winter are good growing conditions. The plants can be grafted to speed up growth when the plants are young, or they can be safely grown on their own roots.

Copiapoas were fashionable about twenty years ago, but they have been less commonly seen in recent times.

BODY

Body shapes fall into two distinct groups: small, spherical bodies forming cushions, or taller and elongated bodies, which usually have a solitary form.

Body colours vary from grey to pale or dark green with shades of brown. A thick tap root is common to many species; ribs are clearly defined whether shallow or deep.

C. cinerea var. *columna-alba*

C. haseltoniana

COPIAPOA

SPINES
Mostly thin, long and brittle. Thick, shorter spines, which are coloured and darker tipped, are also found on some species.

FLOWERS
Large flowers rise centrally from tufts of wool on the crown. The flowers have a short tube; they open wide and the petals are shades of yellow. Many species have perfumed flowers. Flowering can be expected from mid to late summer.

PROPAGATION
Some species can be propagated by offsets, but most plants are grown from seed.

SPECIES
The large number of species which were found and named by Ritter have recently been catalogued — thus adding considerably to the types that are available. The principal species found in collections include *C. applanata*(1), *C. bridgesii*(2), *C. calderana*(2), *C. cinerea columna-alba*(2), *C. coquimbana*(1), *C. echinoides*(1), *C. haseltoniana*(2), *C. humilis*(1), *C. marginata*(2), *C. rubriflora*(2), *C. totoralensis*(1) and *C. tenuissima*(1).

C. cinerea var. *dealbata*

C. humilis

C. hypogaea

C. calderana

C. bridgesii

C. carrizalensis

C. intermedia

CORYPHANTHA (Engelmann) Lemaire

HABITAT
Their natural environment stretches from southern Canada, throughout the United States to as far south as Mexico and Baja California.

Widespread in their natural habitat, the species of the *Coryphantha* genus are smallish in size, spherical to slightly elongated in shape, and are both solitary or branching in habit. Rarely exceeding 25 centimetres in height, these attractive plants deserve attention, as they are easy to grow, flower freely and often have brightly coloured spines.

Typical of this genus are the large flowers that rise from the crown, the furrowed tubercles and the green, glabrous fruits. Attempts to combine species of *Coryphantha* and *Mammillaria* into one genus have resulted in a confusion of names, and the species listed below are sometimes to be found in the *Mammillaria* section of a number of nurseries.

Coryphantha cacti can be successfully grown on their own roots; they will tolerate average conditions with well-drained, coarse soils. They prefer full sun and dry wintering.

BODY
Small in size, often 20–25 centimetres in height, generally spherical to slightly elongated in shape, and soft-bodied with noticeably furrowed tubercles. Green to greyish green in colour. Their pattern of growth is solitary or branching from the base.

SPINES
Radiating spines are usually short, interlacing, and often brittle. The central spines are longer, thicker and often brightly coloured. Spines can be white, light reddish brown or dark brown, with central spines sometimes bent at the tip.

FLOWERS
Blooms rise centrally from a crown, which is covered with tufts of wool; the flowers are large and glossy, white, golden yellow, or red in colour, sometimes with a darker centre.

Flowering occurs from mid to late summer, with many species having to reach maturity before flowering can take place.

C. cornifera

C. asperispina

C. michoacanensis

C. radians

C. longicornis

C. vivipara var. *neomexicana*

PROPAGATION
Seeds are used except for the species that produce basal offsets.

SPECIES
Although numerous species have been classified in their natural habitats, some may be listed as mammillarias: *C. albicolumnaris*, *C. andreae*, *C. asterias*, *C. chlorantha*, *C. clava*, *C. clavata*, *C. cornifera*, *C. cornuta*, *C. densispina*, *C. difficilis*, *C. echinus*, *C. longicornis*, *C. minima*, *C. michoacanensis*, *C. octacantha*, *C. pectinata*, *C. radians*, *C. recurvata*, *C. speciosa*, *C. vaupeliana* and *C. vivipara*.

DENMOZA Britton & Rose

HABITAT
A small genus of hardy cacti from Argentina, these suit a sunny position, a coarse soil mix, ample watering during the summer months, and a dry winter rest.

BODY
The spherical to elongated body becomes columnar with age. A flattened crown in older specimens is typical. Well-defined ribs are grey-green in colour.

SPINES
Dense and long, reddish brown in colour, the spines are interspersed with hair. Central spines are longer, darker coloured and up to 8 centimetres long.

FLOWERS
Flowers are red in colour, with a narrow, long flower tube, which is slightly bent, arising from the crown of older plants. Flowering occurs in late summer.

PROPAGATION
These cacti do not offset easily, so propagation is usually from seed.

SPECIES
Two species have been described:
D. erythrocephala and *D. rhodacantha*.

Denmoza sp.

D. erythrocephala

DISCOCACTUS Pfeiffer

HABITAT
One of the more difficult-to-maintain genera of cacti, *Discocactus* comes from Brazil, Paraguay and Bolivia.

These spherical, slow-growing plants resemble *Melocactus*, though *Discocactus* cephalia are smaller, their flowers are elongated and appear to open at night. They require hot, humid conditions and, like *Melocactus*, do not withstand well the fall in temperatures in winter when they are grown in Europe or other cool climate regions.

An extremely porous, mineral-based soil mix, caution with watering, and high air humidity appear to be essential to these cacti. Loss of roots by older plants is typical, and collectors often resort to grafting *Discocactus* for that reason.

BODY
These cacti are broadly spherical and slow-growing. They develop a cephalium at the apex, from which the flowers arise. Their tubercular ribs are dull green to bluish green in colour. Loss of roots in older plants or those directly imported from their native habitat can be a problem.

The use of a temperature-controlled growing cabinet is recommended. Watering by bottom soaking is best.

SPINES
Attractive and colourful; central spines often cannot be distinguished from radials, as both are well-coloured, from pink to brown, and often darker tipped.

FLOWERS
Flowers arise from the apical cephalium on mature plants. Flowering is nocturnal, and the strongly scented flowers are more or less funnel-form, with a slender, elongated flower tube. In some species, flowers reach 7 to 9 centimetres in length; colour ranges from cream-white to pink. Flowering occurs in mid to late summer.

PROPAGATION
Usually from seed.

SPECIES
D. bahiensis, *D. boomianus*, *D. horstii* and *D. tricornis*.

Discocactus horstii

Discocactus horstii

91

DOLICOTHELE (K. Schumann) Britton & Rose, emended Backeberg

Subgenus of *Mammillaria* according to E. Götz

HABITAT
These cacti come from Texas and Mexico. Often considered to be closely related to *Mammillaria*, they may sometimes be listed as a *Mammillaria* (Britton & Rose), or they may appear as a separate genus, and are listed as such by Buxbaum and Backeberg. Known also as *Dolichotele*.

Attractive and not difficult to maintain, *Dolicothele* flower profusely from an early age. A coarse soil mix, dry winter rest and ample watering during the growing season are recommended. These cacti grow well on their own roots.

BODY
Spherical to slightly elongated, these cacti offset freely to form groups of heads. Elongated tubercles are typical. Spination is yellow to white. The central spines are often hooked and dark tipped, usually flexible and several centimetres long.

FLOWERS
Two distinct groups of species, one small-flowered, the other large-flowered. Flowers are bell-shaped and as in other *Mammillaria* types arise in a ring from axels near the top third of the plant. Usually of creamy white to pale yellow, sometimes with pink stripe, flowers appear from early to late summer.

PROPAGATION
By separating groups of the individual heads, or by seed.

SPECIES
Listed nowadays as a subgenus of *Mammillaria*, the more popular *Dolicothele* include:
D. albescens, *D. baumii*, *D. camptotricha*, *D. longimamma*, *D. sphaerica*, *D. uberiformis* and *D. zephyranthoides.*

D. sphaerica

D. camptotricha

ECHINOCACTUS Link & Otto

HABITAT
Large growing, spherical cacti from the southern states of the United States and Mexico. Their attractive spination and the regular flowering of mature plants make these cacti popular with growers. They require a coarse soil mix, dry winter rest and full sun position. Echinocacti grow well on their own roots.

BODY
Spherical at first, the body becomes elongated with age; some species are cylindrical and reach up to 2 metres in height, and over 1 metre in diameter. In warm climates and frost-free zones they can be grown in outdoor gardens.

SPINES
Stout, long and attractively coloured spines; the central spines project. Spines are yellow to reddish brown in colour, and 5 or more centimetres long.

FLOWERS
Usually golden yellow in colour, 3 to 5 centimetres long, and bell-shaped. Flowering occurs in a ring near the apex in mid to late summer.

PROPAGATION
Seldom offsetting, so propagation is usually from seed.

SPECIES
The following are amongst the most attractive of all spherical cacti: *E. grandis*, *E. grusonii*, *E. ingens*, *E. palmeri*, *E. platyacanthus* and *E. polycephalus*.

E. grusonii

E. ingens

ECHINOCEREUS Engelmann

HABITAT
A large group of short cereoid cacti found in parts of the United States and Mexico.

Extensive variation exists between the many species of *Echinocereus*, as well as between the intermediate types that have been identified. All species are short and cylindrical in shape; they form low groups, have offsets and flower profusely.

These attractive plants, with large colourful flowers, are highly recommended and must rate as one of the most popular cacti with collectors. They are easy to propagate, relatively simple to cultivate and have strikingly beautiful flowers and colourful spines — a combination not often seen in the family of Cactaceae. Dry winter rest and a medium coarse soil mix are recommended. Plants can be grown on their own roots or grafted to increase growth and flowering.

BODY
Short, cylindrical, soft bodies, greyish green in colour. These cacti usually form colonies by offsetting at the base, but offsets are also formed higher up the body. They customarily reach 20 centimetres in height.

SPINES
Short and soft, often pectinate (comb-like), with a great variety of colours. In some species, the longer central spines are darker tipped.

FLOWERS
Very large and attractively coloured. These cacti flower profusely from the sides of the body and near the crown. The flower is large and funnelform, with a characteristic spination and tufts of wool on the buds and at base of the flower tubes.

Colours include mauve and red, often with a darker centre. Flowering can be expected from an early age and continues throughout summer.

PROPAGATION
By offsets, which are easily detached from the mother plant, or from seed.

E. chloranthus

E. palmerii

E. procumbens

SPECIES
A large number of species have been identified and named; a selection of the better known are given: *E. adustus*, *E. albatus*, *E. baileyi*, *E. blanckii*, *E. brandegeei*, *E. conglomeratus*, *E. delaetii*, *E. dubius*, *E. kunzei*, *E. melanocentrus*, *E. octacanthus*, *E. palmerii*, *E. pectinatus*, *E. pentalophus*, *E. procumbens*, *E. roetteri*, *E. salmianus*, *E. scheeri*, *E. tayopensis*, *E. triglochidiatus* and *E. viridiflorus*.

E. viridiflorus var. *davisii*

ECHINOCEREUS

E. marksianus

E. delaetii

E. pectinatus var. rigidissimus

E. species in Lower Sonora Desert

ECHINOFOSSULOCACTUS Lawrence

HABITAT
A very attractive and homogeneous group of plants from northern and central Mexico.

These cacti are easily recognisable and are smallish in size. They are spherical and have many ribs — sometimes up to one hundred on a single plant. The flattened spines are typical of many species.

Given a coarse soil mix, dry winter rest and full exposure to the sun during the growing season, they can be most rewarding to grow. Attractively coloured spines and a perfect symmetry of body form are readily apparent, even in young plants. They do not tolerate excessively dry conditions during their growing period, and misting on hot days is recommended. They can be grown on their own roots or can be grafted.

BODY
Greyish green in colour, with numerous ribs, often thin and wavy in appearance. The plants are relatively small in size and solitary in habit. Only a few species freely produce offsets.

SPINES
Thin and long with interlacing radial spines; the central spines are often thick, coloured and flattened, even blade-like. The colour varies from cream-white to brown.

FLOWERS
Small or medium-sized flowers rise from the crown early in spring. The flower tube is glabrous, white to violet in colour, and often displays a darker stripe. Many species flower at an early age.

PROPAGATION
As a number of the species do not readily form offsets, plants are often propagated from seed.

SPECIES
The more attractive species include: *E. albatus*, *E. arrigens*, *E. confusus*, *E. hastatus*, *E. lloydii*, *E. multicostatus*, *E. ochoterenaus*, *E. tetraxiphus*, *E. vaupelianus*, *E. violaciflorus* and *E. zacatecasensis*.

E. albatus

E. ochoterenaus

ECHINOFOSSULOCACTUS

E. lloydii

E. xiphacanthus

E. arrigens

E. zacatecasensis

ECHINOMASTUS Britton & Rose

Subgenus of *Neolloydia* according to E. Götz

HABITAT
Small, low spherical to short cylindrical cacti from the southern states of the United States and northern Mexico. The cacti of this genus resemble those of *Thelocactus* and have been listed by some authors as a subgenus of *Thelocactus* (Schumann).

A coarse, high-mineral-content soil mix, dry winter rest and cautious watering are required by these plants. They can be difficult to maintain on their own roots, so they are often grafted. They prefer a warm, sunny position.

BODY
These cacti are small, and generally low and spherical, though some species have a cylindrical shape. Rows of fairly well-defined ribs are formed by large tubercles, often with transverse depressions. Pale green to bluish green in colour.

SPINES
Clustered radiating spines, up to eighteen per areole are typical. Central spines are projecting, 2 to 3 centimetres long and coloured from brown to reddish brown.

FLOWERS
Flowers appear in mid-summer. They are small to medium-sized, up to 3 centimetres long and bell-shaped. Flowers arise in a ring near the apex. They are pale red or pink to light purple in colour.

PROPAGATION
Usually by seed.

SPECIES
Those seen in collections include, *E. acumensis*, *E. intertextus*, *E. johnsonnii*, *E. kakui*, *E. macdowellii*, *E. mariposensis* and *E. unguispinus*.

E. macdowellii

99

ECHINOPSIS Zuccarini

HABITAT

The natural distribution of *Echinopsis* extends from northern Bolivia, Argentina, Uruguay and Paraguay to southern Brazil.

One of the earliest of all the cactus genera to be described was the *Echinopsis*. Initially (1837) classified as a combination of several genera — *Echinopsis*, *Trichocereus*, *Lobivia* and *Pseudolobivia* — it has now been accepted that these widely differing groups should be separated and classified under their own generic names. This separation was held to be valid for a number of physiological as well as geographical reasons, notwithstanding the fact that it is clearly obvious from an examination of these plants that a common ancestral type exists for all of them, and for all the intermediate types that are known to exist.

The plants classified as *Echinopsis* are generally spherical at first; with age they become elongated, at which stage they attain a short cereoid shape. The differences between the shape of the flowers are seen from the description of *Echinopsis* given here, and from the similar genera discussed under their individual names.

The *Echinopsis* cacti are hardy plants and well suited to outdoor culture. A sunny position, dry winter rest, and a fertile coarse soil mix will promote good growth and encourage more prolific flowering. These plants grow successfully on their own roots.

E. mamilosa var. *kermesina*

E. coronata

E. ancistrophora forma *cristata*

E. Paramount hybrid group

E. multiplex

E. multiplex (flower detail)

ECHINOPSIS

BODY
Spherical at first, the bodies later become elongated, attaining a columnar shape and reaching up to 1 metre in height. Colours vary from green to greyish green. Offsets are typical in many species.

SPINES
Thick, usually short, of light colour with central spines longer and often dark tipped.

FLOWERS
Longer and broader than the flowers of related genera. The *Echinopsis* flower is generally funnelform and opens during the day, or, sometimes, at night only. Colours are attractive and range from white to shades of red; the flowers have a strong scent. Flowering occurs from mid to late summer.

Some species flower at an early age, others after reaching maturity. Removing the offsets improves flowering. More prolific flowering is associated with *Echinopsis* hybrids (*Echinopsis* × *Trichocereus* and similar crosses).

PROPAGATION
Separated offsets form roots easily. Large-scale propagation is from seed.

SPECIES
After separating the *Trichocereus*, *Lobivia* and *Pseudolobivia* genera from *Echinopsis*, two dozen named *Echinopsis* species remain. They include the generally more popular *E. baldiana*, *E. brasiliensis*, *E. calochlora*, *E. chacoana*, *E. eyriesii*, *E. grandiflora*, *E. haku-jomaru*, *E. leucantha*, *E. mamillosa*, *E. multiplex*, *E. rhodotricha*, *E. schaferi*, *E. silverstrii*, *E. turbinata* and *E. werdermanii*.

E. hybrid: 'sunset'

E. hybrid: 'red pygmy'

E. haku-jomaru

E. rhodotricha

E. hybrid: 'stars and stripes'

E. obrepanda var. *purpurosea*

ENCEPHALOCARPUS Berger

HABITAT
Small, spherical cacti from Mexico.

These slow-growing cacti are usually grafted to speed up the growth of young seedlings. They require full sun, a warm position, dry winter rest and cautious watering. A well-drained porous soil mix with a high mineral content is recommended.

BODY
Small, depressed spherical shape and enlarged tap root. Distinctive wool growth in apex; ribs formed by tubercles; sparse spination on the youngest tubercles near the plant's top.

FLOWERS
The relatively large flowers — up to 3 centimetres long — are deeply coloured in violet-red. Flowers arise on a short tube from tufts of wool on the apex. The fruits form within the apical wool. Flowering is in mid-summer.

PROPAGATION
Usually by seed.

SPECIES
Single species described, *E. strobiliformis*.

E. strobiliformis

EPIPHYLLOPSIS (Berger) Backeberg & Knuth

Subgenus of *Schlumbergera* according to E. Götz

HABITAT
A variable group of species from Brazilian forest. Various divergent characteristics in the morphology of *Epiphyllopsis* flowers and segments can be attributed to the environment from which the collected plants came, usually the amount of direct sunlight received.

These are epiphytic cacti that require a humus-rich soil mix, regular watering, diffused light and a hardening period of reduced moisture and temperature during winter. Misting in the warmer summer months is recommended.

BODY
The segmented stem has occasional bristles on mature segments, forming shrubs with flowering from apical segments. *Epiphyllopsis* is not unlike *Zygocactus*, but differs in the morphology of the flowers and longer segments. They are usually grown on their own roots and in hanging baskets.

FLOWERS
Free-flowering, especially if a soil mix enriched with leaf mulch and nitrogen is used, and the plants spend some time in summer outdoors in a partially shaded area. The flowers appear from the end segments, sometimes in groups. The flowers are regular in structure, have a short tube and a five-angled ovary. The flowers are 4 centimetres long and bright red in colour. Flowering occurs in early to mid summer.

PROPAGATION
Easily propagated by separating the mature segments and rooting them in a growing soil mix at high humidity.

SPECIES
Only one species has been described, *E. gaertnerii*.

E. gaertnerii

EPIPHYLLUM Haworth

HABITAT
One of the earliest described leafy cacti, these epiphytic cacti are widespread in their natural habitats, ranging from Mexico to many countries of subtropical South America and the West Indies.

Long, thin segments and nocturnal large and glabrous flowers are typical. A soil mix enriched with leaf mulch, a warm position of diffused light, and ample watering during the growing season are recommended. Flowering will be increased — as with all epiphytes — if these cacti are placed outdoors for some time during summer. They are usually grown on their own roots.

BODY
A long, strongly growing body, with thin segments free of spination. Some species have greater lobe development than others.

FLOWERS
Large flowers, up to 20 centimetres long, may be even longer in some hybrids. Flowers are usually white and may be scented; they open at night. The flower is glabrous and has a thin and long flower tube. The fruit is oblong. Well-grown plants flower profusely.

PROPAGATION
Individual segments are separated and rooted in a growing soil mix.

SPECIES
Dozens of excellent hybrids are in cultivation. From the naturally occurring species the following show merit in cultivation: *E. cartagense*, *E. caulorhizum*, *E. crenatum*, *E. grandilobum*, *E. hookeri*, *E. macrocarpum*, *E. phyllanthus*, *E. ruestii* and *E. strictum*.

E. ackermannii

E. grandilobum

EPITHELANTHA Weber ex Britton & Rose

Subgenus of *Mammillaria* according to E. Götz

HABITAT
Small spherical to slightly elongated cacti that resemble cacti of the genus *Mammillaria* apart from the fact that *Epithelantha*'s flowers do not arise from axils of mature tubercles in a familiar ring below the apex, but rather grow from the youngest areoles on the apex. In the lime-rich soils of their native Texas to northern Mexico, these cacti branch freely to form groups of heads. The enlarged tap root is sensitive to excess moisture, and grafted plants are common in collections. A coarse, well-drained soil mix, with gypsum added is recommended. Dry winter rest and a sunny position are preferred.

BODY
Small spherical to slightly elongated, or short cylindrical in shape. Tubercles are small, arranged in spirals, sometimes in ribs. Large tap root typical.

SPINES
Dense spination. The short spines, greyish to white, largely conceal the body. Some central spines near the crown are longer and projecting.

FLOWERS
Small, whitish to pink-red flowers arise from the young areoles on top in mid-summer.

PROPAGATION
By separating offsets or by seed.

SPECIES
Species seen in many collections are *E. micromeris*, *E. pachyrhiza* and *E. polycephala*.

E. micromeris var. *tuberosa*

E. micromeris

ERDISIA Britton & Rose

HABITAT
Slim cereoid cacti, more or less upright, with long
spination and funnelform flowers, native to
southern Peru and Chile. These cacti grow well
on their own roots in a coarse soil mix, with
minimal watering during winter rest. A sunny,
warm position is recommended. Also known as
Corryocactus.

BODY
With slim, cereoid stems of up to 1 to 2 metres
long, these cacti are either more upright or
prostrate to ascending, depending on the species.
Ribs are clearly defined, and shoots tend toward a
cylindrical shape in the less upright species.
Bluish green in colour.

SPINES
Attractive, well-coloured spines. Central spines,
up to 6 centimetres long, are projecting; radials,
thin and spreading.

FLOWERS
Funnelform, yellow to orange-flame and bright
red in colour, up to 5 centimetres long. Flowers
are usually borne on the flanks, and a dense
bristly growth forms at the flower tube base.
Flowering is in mid to late summer.

PROPAGATION
Cuttings from stems or by seed.

SPECIES
From those seen most often in collection the
following are of interest: *E. aureispina*, *E. erecta*,
E. maxima, *E. ruthae* and *E. spiniflora*.

Erdisia sp. nov. (Menrath)

ERIOCACTUS Backeberg

Subgenus of *Notocactus* according to E. Götz

HABITAT
A genus of cacti closely related to *Notocactus*; both genera are native to Brazil and Paraguay.

Eriocactus species, broadly spherical cacti that become elongated with age, are amongst the most attractive, easy-to-maintain and freely flowering of all the cacti, and they deserve more attention by collectors. They grow well on their own roots in a well-drained soil mix of medium coarseness. Full sun exposure and regular watering during the growing season, with a dry winter rest, are recommended.

BODY
The bluish green body becomes cylindrical and elongated with age, when it has a distinctively flattened, wool-covered apex, which inclines toward sun. Ribs are numerous, shallow and slightly tuberculate.

SPINES
Fine, bristly and dense spines virtually cover the body. Downward-pointed central spines are longer. All spines are golden to cream coloured; in some species spines tend toward brownish red, with centrals darker tipped.

E. leninghausii

E. leninghausii var. *cristata*

ERIOCACTUS

E. magnificus

E. schumannianus

FLOWERS
Large, funnelform and wider than they are long, flowers are up to 6 centimetres diameter. The flower tube has dense brown wool. The pale yellow flowers appear from early to mid-summer.

PROPAGATION
These cacti rarely offset, so propagation is usually from seed.

SPECIES
From the handful named, the following are most attractive: *E. leninghausii*, *E. magnificus* and *E. schumannianus*.

ERIOCEREUS (Berger) Riccobono

HABITAT
Climbing or prostrate cerei from Argentina, Brazil, Paraguay and Uruguay, used for grafting stock by many collectors and nurseries specialising in cacti. In their native habitat, *Eriocereus* cacti reach great heights of several metres and have large, nocturnal flowers.

Eriocereus are seen in larger glasshouses or in warmer gardens in frost-free climates. The larger plants require support. They prefer a coarse soil mix, ample watering during the growing season, and a dry winter rest. Seedlings are rapid-growing and reach grafting size quickly (*E. jusbertii*).

E. justbertii

BODY
Cereoid and green to bluish green colour. These cacti are more or less upright, and support is needed for taller plants. Ribs are clearly defined but few in number, and they often branch from the base. These cacti grow well on their own roots.

SPINES
Short, stout spines; the centrals are up to 4 centimetres long in some species and are sometimes darker tipped. Yellow-brown in colour in young plants.

FLOWERS
Large and up to 25 centimetres long, flowers are funnelform in shape, nocturnal, and white in colour. Fruit is red. Flowering occurs after the cactus has reached mature size. Flowering occurs from mid to late summer.

PROPAGATION
Propagation is by separating the stems at the base or by seed.

SPECIES
These cacti are not commonly seen in collections apart from the useful grafting stock *E. jusbertii*. Other common species include *E. adscendens*, *E. martinii*, *E. regelii* and *E. tephracanthus*.

E. tephracanthus

ESCOBARIA Britton & Rose

Subgenus of *Mammillaria* according to E. Götz

HABITAT
Small spherical to cylindrical cacti from the
southern states of the United States and Mexico.

Many species are freely offsetting and form
large colonies of heads. A coarse soil mix, a
sunny, warm position and a dry winter rest are
important. Mature plants can be difficult to
maintain on their own roots, so these cacti often
are grafted. Many species are, however, happy on
their own roots.

BODY
Spherical at first, these cacti later become
elongated or cylindrical in shape. They have
clearly defined tubercles, like the closely related
genus of *Coryphantha*. Freely offsetting to form
groups.

SPINES
Dense, sharp, thin spines. The central spine is
often longer and brightly coloured, sometimes
darker tipped.

FLOWERS
Small flowers, up to 3 centimetres in diameter,
arise from the apex. They can be brightly
coloured, depending on the species, ranging from
creamy white to pink or deeper red and tending
toward purple. Elongated berries are similar to
those of *Mammillaria*. Flowering occurs in early
to mid-summer.

PROPAGATION
From offsets or by seed.

SPECIES
A number of species are sometimes listed under
related genera, such as *Coryphantha*, *Neobesseya*
and *Neolloydia*. Those seen in collections
include *E. albicolumnaria*, *E. bella*,
E. chihuahuensis, *E. hesteri*, *E. lloydii*,
E. neomexicana, *E. orcuttii*, *E. rigida*,
E. tuberculosa, *E. roseana* and *E. varicolor*.

E. alamoensis

E. runyonii

E. chaffeyii

E. gigantea

ESPOSTOA Britton & Rose

Including *Pseudoespostoa* Backeberg

HABITAT

Two closely related genera of tall, columnar cacti from Peru and southern Ecuador. The natural distribution of both the plants is restricted to the higher altitudes of the Andes, 1000 to 2400 metres above sea level.

The separation of these two genera is not recognised by all collectors, though some significant differences in seeds, growth patterns and most importantly, the formation of the flowering zone — the cephalium — can be observed.

The taller-growing *Espostoa* forms a shrub by branching from the sides well above ground level. *Espostoa* seeds are without lustre, and the cephalium is formed in a deep groove in the plant's apex. The woolly, hair-like growth that covers the plant is less dense than that of *Pseudoespostoa* and is somewhat coarse.

The *Pseudoespostoa* genus includes plants that branch haphazardly from the base, have shiny seeds and a finer, cotton-wool-like apical hair that is denser than that of *Espostoa*. The cephalium of *Pseudoespostoa* does not rise from a deep groove, but resembles the 'artificial' cephalium of the *Cephalocereus*.

The tall and majestic *Espostoa* plants are often the crowning glory of a garden or glasshouse. Their white, hair-covered columns can develop to a full height of several metres.

These are slow-growing plants, and grafting can be used to speed up the growth of young seedlings. They prefer a deep, coarse soil mix, a sheltered position, and, if grown outside, they may require protection from frosts.

BODY

Tall, columnar plants, branching either from the base or sides. The body is divided into numerous ribs. It is slow-growing and covered with a more or less dense wool growth, which resembles long, white hair. The density of hair cover increases near the apex.

E. mirabilis FR 670

E. ritterii forma *cristata*

114

E. ritterii forma *cristata*

ESPOSTOA Britton & Rose

E. lanata

E. lanata (flowering zone)

SPINES
The radiating spines are fairly short and yellow-white in colour. The centrals are often longer, projecting through the wool; they are bone coloured or browny red. In some species the central spines are very thick and long.

FLOWERS
Espostoa plants have a deep groove or cleft near the apex, which is clearly marked. The cephalium itself consists of a longer, bristly growth that is considerably more dense than the surrounding wool.

Pseudoespostoa plants have a flower zone formed by a shallow 'artificial' cephalium. The flowers vary in length and are nocturnal. The flower tube is hairy, white to yellow in colour, and the fruits of the *Espostoa*, when ripe, are red; those of the *Pseudoespostoa* are white. Flower-bearing cephaliums develop on mature plants in mid to late summer.

PROPAGATION
This genus can be propagated from offsets, by the mother plant system, or from seed.

SPECIES
Species classified as *Espostoa* include *E. huanucensis*, *E. lanata*, *E. mirabilis*, *E. mocupensis*, *E. procera* and *E. ritterii*. Species classified as *Pseudoespostoa* include *P. melanostele* and *P. nana*.

EULYCHNIA Philippi

HABITAT
Cereoid, freely branching cacti from northern Chile, these reach several metres in height.

Fierce spination, areolar wool and bell-shaped flowers are typical. These are hardy plants, well suited to a sunny position, coarse soil mix, and a dry winter rest. They are usually grown on their own roots.

BODY
The cereoid-shaped body has well-defined ribs; it branches above, reaching tree-like proportions of up to 7 metres in height. Grey-green to fresh green in colour.

SPINES
Fierce, grey-brown radials and protruding, long centrals to 15 centimetres long. Areolar wool typical near the apex.

FLOWERS
Bell-shaped flowers. The flowering zone has noticeable areolar wool, white to brown in colour. The flower tube is short. Large flowers, reaching 7 to 8 centimetres long are white to pale pink in colour. Fruits are covered in hair. Flowering occurs in late summer.

PROPAGATION
Usually by seed.

SPECIES
From the handful described, the following are of interest: *E. acida*, *E. aricensis FR 197*, *E. procumbens*, *E. ritterii* and *E. saint-pieana FR 497a*.

E. ritterii

FEROCACTUS Britton & Rose

Subgenus of *Echinocactus* according to
L. Benson.

HABITAT
A large group of broadly spherical to cylindrical
or barrel-shaped cacti from the deserts of the
southern states of the United States and Mexico.

These cacti often offset from the base to form
large groups, or they may be solitary, in which
case they may reach a height of up to 4 metres.
Their attractive spination and body form, both of
which are brightly coloured, and easy
maintenance mean that these cacti deserve
attention from all growers. They prefer a coarse
soil mix, sunny position and ample watering
during the growth period, as well as dry winter
rest. *Ferocactus* species grow well on their own
roots.

BODY
Although the body is usually large and barrel-
shaped, some species are more freely offsetting
and form cushions with spherical heads. Greyish
green in colour.

SPINES
Stout, thick and brightly coloured spines; the
central spines reach 10 or more centimetres in
length and are sometimes hooked. The spines are
yellow to brown-red.

F. schwarzii

F. latispinus

F. orcutii

F. echidne

F. pilosus

F. fordii

FEROCACTUS

F. coloratus

F. tortulospinus

FLOWERS
Flowering usually occurs in mature plants that reach a large size. The flowers, which appear in late summer are typically scaly, glabrous and relatively short, coloured yellow to shades of red. They arise in a ring near the apex.

PROPAGATION
By separating offsets or by seed.

SPECIES
From the large number classified the following attractive species demand attention:
F. acanthodes, F. coloratus, F. echidne, F. flavovirens, F. gatesii, F. glaucescens, F. haematacanthus, F. histrix, F. horridus, F. latispinus, F. macrodiscus, F. recurvus, F. robustus, F. schwarzii, F. stainesii, F. viridescens and *F. wislizenii.*

F. acanthodes

FRAILEA Britton & Rose

HABITAT
A group of small, spherical cacti from Brazil, Uruguay, Bolivia, Argentina and Paraguay, as well as limited habitats in Colombia.

An easy-to-maintain genus, *Frailea* are suited to a coarse soil mix and sunny position. They need ample watering during the growing season and a dry winter rest. *Frailea* grow well on their own roots, though they are sometimes grafted to increase flowering. Cleistogamic flowers, which often form seeds without opening, are typical.

BODY
The small, spherical body becomes rectangular with age. Low ribs are formed by rows of tubercles, which are green to light brown in colour. Older or grafted plants offset freely.

SPINES
Short, bristly spines. White to horn colour or reddish brown. Central spines are slightly longer and projecting.

FLOWERS
Flowers arise from the central apex during hot periods in late summer. Often the flowers do not open, and they form seeds in a self-fertile fashion. Flowers are funnelform, and yellow or greenish white to reddish brown. The flower tube is covered with a distinctive brown wool.

PROPAGATION
Usually grown from seed, these cacti rapidly reach flowering size. Seed is distinctively 'hat'-shaped.

SPECIES
From the large number described the following are seen in many collections: *F. albicolumnaris*, *F. albifusca FR 1392*, *F. asperispina FR 1368*, *F. aureispina FR 1386*, *F. castanea*, *F. colombiana*, *F. deminuta*, *F. fulviseta*, *F. knippeliana*, *F. pullispina*, *F. pygmaea* and *F. schilinzkyana*.

F. itapuyensis

F. sp. nov. *FR 1112* (Ritter)

F. pumila

FRAILEA

F. schilinzkyana

F. asterioides

F. asterioides forma cristata

GLANDULICACTUS Backeberg

Subgenus of *Echinocactus* according to
L. Benson.

HABITAT
A distinct group of species of spherical shape
from the deserts of Mexico and the southern
states of the United States.

Tuberculate ribs, elongated areoles and brightly
coloured spination are typical. A coarse soil mix,
cautious watering and a dry winter rest are
important, and a sunny warm position is
preferred. Usually grafted.

BODY
A spherical to slightly rectangular body, which
becomes slightly elongated with age. Tuberculate
ribs and elongated areoles. Bluish green colour.
Older plants can be difficult to maintain on their
own roots.

SPINES
Stout, brightly coloured central spines, up to 10
centimetres long and hooked. Radial spines are
shorter. Spines are straw to reddish yellow in
colour.

FLOWERS
The small flowers, about 2 centimetres long, are
more or less funnelform, with a short tube. They
open only partly and are purple to brownish red
in colour. Flowering occurs in early summer.

PROPAGATION
Usually by seed.

SPECIES
Two species have been described,
G. crassihamatus and *G. uncinatus.*

G. uncinatus

G. uncinatus var. *wrightii*

GYMNOCACTUS Backeberg

Subgenus of *Neolloydia* according to E. Götz

HABITAT
Small, spherical cacti, closely related to *Turbinicarpus*, from north-east Mexico.

Low, tuberculate ribs, with a naked flower tube and fruits are typical. A coarse soil mix, cautious watering and dry winter rest are important for these cacti. They are sometimes grafted, especially the species that have distinct root restriction, as these can be difficult to maintain. A warm, sunny position recommend.

BODY
The body is small and spherical, and bluish green in colour. Individual plants can be up to 6 to 8 centimetres in diameter. Some species offset to form cushions of heads. Elongated areoles and small tubercles are typical. The apex is slightly woolly.

SPINES
Fine spination occurs in most species. Radial spines are short. In some species, the central spines are longer; they may be up to 2 centimetres long and darker than the radials. Spines are yellow to brown in colour, and are sometimes curved.

FLOWERS
Medium-sized flowers are close to 3 centimetres long, with a naked tube and ovary. Flowers are usually purple. Flowering occurs in mid to late summer.

PROPAGATION
Separating individual offsets or in solitary species by seed.

SPECIES
Some of the more attractive species include *G. beguinnii, G. horripilus, G. knuthianus, G. subterraneus* and *G. viereckii.*

G. horripilus

G. knuthianus

G. goldii

GYMNOCALYCIUM Pfeiffer

HABITAT

Gymnocalycium is a large and extensively cultivated genus of cacti from Bolivia, Paraguay, Uruguay, southern Brazil and Argentina. It was first mentioned as a separate genus in 1845, and since then it has become one of the most popular cacti with growers in all countries.

These are hardy plants of small to medium size and spherical shape. The tuberculate ribs, glabrous flowers, and the fruits with their distinctive scales are typical of all *Gymnocalycium* species.

Usually these cacti do not demand special attention or a particular soil type, though winter rest and a semi-shaded position on the cooler side of a glasshouse — as well as plentiful watering during the growing season — are recommended. They can be grafted, although they also grow well on their own roots.

G. andreae var. *grandiflorum*

BODY

A very small to medium-sized body, always spherical and becoming slightly elongated with age. The body is formed by rows of tuberculate ribs that are more or less defined, depending on the species. The body colours range from greyish green to variegated shades of green and reddish brown.

Natural mutation under cultivation in Japan has, in recent times, produced plants that lack chlorophyll — the so-called red ball cactus or the *G. mihanovichii* mutant — which has to be grafted in order to survive. Some species offset freely; others do not.

G. baldianum

SPINES

Variation in both colour and size is great. Spines can be curved close to the body, often interlacing and projecting to form a dense cover. Some varieties have short and straight spines; others have longer centrals, which are attractively coloured in yellow, brown, or shades of red.

G. deeszianum

GYMNOCALYCIUM

FLOWERS
Most species flower freely from early to late summer, even at an early age. Flowers rise from top of the tubercles, near the areole, and have scales on the flower tube and buds. The flowers vary in size from very large to small; they have slender tubes, are funnelform in shape, and occur in many attractive colours, ranging from white and yellow to pink and red. Glabrous fruits are typical.

PROPAGATION
More usually from seed, but they can be raised from offsets if small numbers of plants are required.

SPECIES
From the great number of attractive species the following are most often found in collections:
G. andreae, G. anisitsii, G. asterium, G. baldianum, G. bicolor, G. bodenbenderianum, G. bruchii, G. cardenasianum, G. damsii, G. denudatum, G. gibbosum, G. griseo-pallidum, G. hamatum, G. horridispinum, G. hossei, G. hybopleurum, G. kozelskyanum, G. leeanum, G. mihanovichii, G. multiflorum, G. mostii, G. ochoterenai, G. quehlianum, G. saglione, G. spegazzinii, G. stuckertii, G. vatteri, and *G. zegarrae.*

G. valnicekianum

G. saglione var. *tilcarensis*

G. bruchii

G. hoseii

G. horstii var. *bueneckerii*

G. damsii var. *tucavocense*

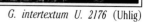

G. intertextum U. 2176 (Uhlig)

GYMNOCALYCIUM

G. mihanovichii var. *friedrichii*

G. leeanum

G. mostii

G. mostii var. *kurtzianum*

G. marquezii var. *argetinense U. 2166* (Uhlig)

G. calochlorum var. *roseiacanthum*

G. quehlianum var. *zantnerianum*

G. millaresii

GYMNOCEREUS Backeberg

Subgenus of *Browningia* according to E. Götz

HABITAT
Tree-like, branching cerei from northern Peru.

These cacti are deep green in colour, and have branches with low, tuberculate ribs and dense areoles, especially near the tip. Long, flexible spines, and nocturnal, glabrous fruits are typical. They grow well on their own roots in a coarse, well-drained soil mix, and need ample watering in the growing season and a dry winter rest. *Gymnocereus* make an attractive contribution to outdoor gardens in frost-free areas.

BODY
Tall, cereoid and branching from sides. In their native habitat *Gymnocereus* species can reach 5 to 6 metres in height. Low ribs and flexible spination typical. Deep green colour and brownish spination.

FLOWERS
The relatively small flowers, 5 to 6 centimetres long, are nocturnal, and white to horn coloured. The glabrous tube is slightly perfumed. Flowering occurs in mid to late summer on mature branches near the tip after the cactus has reached mature height.

PROPAGATION
Usually from seed.

SPECIES
The following are most often seen in collections: *G. altissimus*, *G. amstutziae* and *G. microspermus*.

G. microspermus

Reproduced with permission from Curt Backeberg, *CACTUS LEXICON, Enumeratio diagnostica Cactacearum*, Cassell.

HAAGEOCEREUS Backeberg

HABITAT
Haageocereus are native to the Pacific side of the
Peruvian Andes, where they grow at low altitudes.

A large group of cereoid species, some
Haageocereus cacti are more upright than others;
many are reclining and prostrate in growth. The
attractive spination is dense and well coloured.
As in most cacti, spination develops best in
plants grown outdoors; under these conditions
spines will be longer and denser. A coarse soil
mix, dry wintering and plenty of moisture during
the growing season are recommended. An
outdoor position for even part of the summer will
promote the development of colourful, dense
spines and more plentiful flowers. These cacti
grow well on their own roots.

H. decumbens

BODY
Bushy and cereoid, with numerous low ribs.
These cacti often have a creeping or prostrate
habit, though some species are more upright, and
will grow up to 1 to 2 metres high.

SPINES
Dense and attractively coloured spines, the
colours ranging from golden to brown, and often
lighter on young branches. Both robust and fine
spination are known amongst the species. Central
spines are projecting, and longer and darker,
sometimes black-tipped. Spines can be up to 5 to
6 centimetres long on cacti grown outdoors, but
spines will be shorter on glasshouse cacti.

H. multangularis

SPECIES
Nearly fifty species have been described, amongst
which the following are highly recommended for
all collections: *H. acanthocladus, H. akersii,
H. aureispinus, H. chrysacanthus, H. clavispinus,
H. decumbens, H. dichromus, H. icosagonoides,
H. litoralis, H. multangularis, H. multicolorispinus,
H. platinospinum, H. pseudomelanostele,
H. rubrospinus, H. salmonoideus, H. versicolor*
and *H. viridiflorus.*

FLOWERS
The large, funnelform flowers are usually
coloured in shades of white or red. Flowers are
nocturnal, and the fruits, oval in shape, are
always hairy. Flowering occurs in mid-summer.

PROPAGATION
By sections of individual stems or by seed.

HAMATOCACTUS Britton & Rose

Subgenus of *Echinocactus* according to L. Benson

HABITAT
A genus of small, spherical cacti from Texas and northern Mexico.

All species have narrow ribs slightly swollen around the areoles, and large, glossy yellow flowers. The plants are easy to grow and prefer a coarse soil mix, full sun and winter rest without watering. They can be grown on their own roots, and flowering can be expected in young plants.

BODY
The small, spherical body, green to greyish green in colour, becomes slightly elongated with age. Clearly defined, narrow ribs. The plants rarely offset, except when the growing tip becomes damaged.

SPINES
Thin and bristly, the central spines are longer, lighter tipped and off-white in colour. Some central spines are always hooked and are slightly reddish; radial spines are straight.

FLOWERS
The large flowers appear in attractive shades of golden yellow with a sheen. Some flowers have a red centre. Buds are green, scaly, and rise from the top of areoles near the crown. Flowering occurs in quite young plants in mid-summer. Flowers are 5 to 7 centimetres long and open fully to a diameter of over 6 centimetres.

PROPAGATION
By seed, because unless the plant is grafted or damaged, offsets rarely form.

SPECIES
From the handful of *Hamatocactus* that have been classified the following are the best known: *H. hamatacanthus*, *H. setispinus* and *H. sinuatus*.

H. chihuahuaensis

H. hamatacanthus

H. setispinus

HARRISIA Britton

HABITAT
Shrub-forming cerei from the West Indies, these cacti closely resemble *Eriocereus*.

Grown usually on their own roots, the semi-upright, high-branching stems of *Harrisia* are night-flowering and require support. They are well-suited to larger glasshouses or an outdoor position of full sun. They prefer a coarse soil mix, regular summer watering and a dry winter rest.

BODY
Tall-growing, branching shrub with a trunk-like base. Fine ribs, with short spination and brown hairs in the flowering zone.

H. tortuosa

FLOWERS
Night-flowering, large, white and often perfumed, the flowers can be up to 15 centimetres long. Flowering occurs from mid to late summer. Orange fruits are typical.

PROPAGATION
Usually by rooting sections of mature stems, or by seed.

SPECIES
The following species are seen in collections: *H. aboriginum*, *H. brookii*, *H. gracilis* and *H. hurstii*.

HELIANTHOCEREUS Backeberg

Subgenus of *Trichocereus* according to W. Rausch

HABITAT
Native to northern Argentina and Bolivia, these cereoid cacti, closely related to the genus *Trichocereus*, are popular with growers on account of their brightly coloured, large flowers and hardy nature. Some of the low-growing, freely branching species are sometimes listed as *Lobivia*, others as *Trichocereus*.

Classification problems aside, these are attractive and easy-to-maintain cacti, well-suited to outdoor gardens. They grow well in sunny positions, without grafting, in a coarse soil mix. Plentiful watering during the growing and flowering seasons, as well as dry over-wintering, are recommended.

BODY
Two groups of species. The members of the first (1), from the higher altitudes, resemble *Trichocereus* in their more solitary, stout and upright growth, as well as their cream-coloured, large funnelform flowers. In the second (2), lower-growing group, are many fine plants, with slender, less-upright stems, coloured spination and diurnal, brightly coloured flowers. Both groups always branch from the base. Low ribs and prostrate growth are typical for some smaller species.

SPINES
Usually dense spination, with stout spines. The central spines are projecting, noticeably longer, and brightly coloured, from straw yellow to darker reddish brown.

FLOWERS
Large, broadly funnelform flowers; some are pale cream to white in colour, others, bright red to yellow. They are always diurnal and have a hairy tube. The solitary, taller species (1) flower near the apex; the lower-branching species flower from the sides all along the stems (2). The fruit is covered by dense brown hair. Flowering is from early to late summer.

H. huascha

PROPAGATION
By separating individual stems or by seed.

SPECIES
Amongst those named are some of the most freely flowering cacti in collections: *H. atacamensis* (1), *H. crassicaulis* (2), *H. grandiflorus* (2), *H. herzogianus* (1), *H. huascha* (2), *H. hyalacanthus* (2), *H. orurensis* (1), *H. pasacana* (1), *H. pecheretianus* (2), *H. poco* (1) and *H. pseudocandicans*.

HERTRICHOCEREUS Backeberg

Subgenus of *Stenocereus* according to E. Götz

HABITAT
Mexican cacti of prostrate, cereoid shape and growth form, they have at times been placed within the genera *Ritterocereus* or *Stenocereus*.

A naked ovary and spiny fruits are typical, as well as a spreading growth habit. These hardy plants grow well in full sun, a coarse soil mix and without watering in winter. They grow well on their own roots.

BODY
Cereoid stems that grow semi-upright to prostrate in shape and branch freely to form a low bush. Well-defined low ribs with elongated tubercles and bluish coating on epidermis.

SPINES
Short radiating spines and downward-pointing longer centrals, up to 5 centimetres long. Reddish brown to grey-brown in colour.

FLOWERS
The large flowers are up to 8 centimetres long and 6 centimetres wide. They are white to pale reddish in colour, and appear from early to mid-summer. Fruits are spiny and reddish in colour.

PROPAGATION
Separating offsets or by seed.

SPECIES
Only one species has been described, *H. beneckei*.

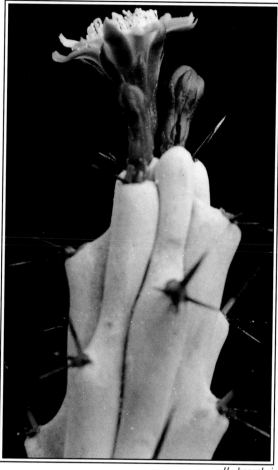

H. beneckei

HOMALOCEPHALA Britton & Rose

Subgenus of *Echinocactus* according to L. Benson

HABITAT
Slow-growing, broadly spherical desert cacti from the southern states of the United States and Mexico.

Attractive for their well-defined geometrical arrangements of ribs and spination, these cacti are also easy to maintain on their own roots. They require a coarse soil mix, dry winter rest and a sunny position. The bright red fruits persist for long time, and often dry up on the plant without opening.

BODY
Broadly spherical, these cacti grow slowly to reach a large size of 40 centimetres in diameter. Greyish green in colour.

SPINES
Stout spines project and sometimes are bent downward. The central spines are brightly coloured, flattened and hooked at the tip, hence the popular name 'horse crippler'. Yellow to reddish in colour, the spines are sometimes banded.

FLOWERS
Bell-shaped flowers can be up to 5 centimetres in diameter. They are bright red to orange in colour, and the fruits are bright red. Flowers arise from the centre in early to mid-summer.

PROPAGATION
This cactus rarely offsets, so propagation is usually from seed.

SPECIES
One species has been described, *H. texensis*.

H. texensis

HORRIDOCACTUS Backeberg

Subgenus of *Neoporteria* according to E. Götz

HABITAT
One of the groups of species of Chilean cacti that at different times and by different authors have been united or separated under various generic names. Ritter's *Pyrrhocactus* and *Chileorebutia* and Backeberg's *Neoporteria* and *Neochilenia* all belong to this group. The modern approach has been to unite these plants of variable morphology and geographical distribution under the name *Neoporteria*, where many of the species listed here can be found in other books. The recognition of *Horridocactus* as a separate genus here is based largely on the more or less glabrous flowers and absence of hair growth on the flower tube. The flower arrangement is said to be also significantly different from that of *Neoporteria* (see under *Neoporteria*). The geographical separation from *Neochilenia*, namely, the barrier of the Andes, is another reason cited by Backeberg (1966) for this new name. (See also under *Neochilenia*.)

    Horridocactus species are mainly solitary, slightly elongated plants (though they are spherical when young) that reach a height of up to 30 centimetres. These cacti are easy to maintain on their own roots in a coarse, well-drained soil mix and in a sunny position. Dry winter rest is important.

BODY
Spherical to broadly spherical at first, these cacti become elongated with age. The broad ribs are more or less tuberculate, depending on the species. Greyish green to bluish green in colour, these cacti do not usually offset freely.

SPINES
Stout, projecting and brightly coloured spines. The prominent central spines are bent and up to 8 centimetres long. Spines are dark brown to black in colour. Dense, fierce-looking spination of plants is typical.

H. paucicostatus FR 493

H. robustus var. *vagasanus*

HORRIDOCACTUS

H. sp. nov. (Ritter)

FLOWERS

Large, more or less glabrous, flowers; no hair on
the flower tube. Flowers reach 6 centimetres in
length and diameter; they are yellow, reddish to
carmine red, often with a lighter coloured stripe.
Flowers arise in mid to late summer from the
apex.

PROPAGATION

Usually by seed.

SPECIES

H. armatus, H. atroviridis, H. curvispinus,
H. echinus, H. paucicostatus, H. robustus and
H. tubericulcatus.

ISLAYA Backeberg

Subgenus of *Neoporteria* according to E. Götz

HABITAT
A group of spherical to elongated cacti from the Pacific region of southern Peru and Chile.

A coarse soil mix, dry winter rest and sunny position suit these cacti well. They are often grafted, as older plants can be difficult to keep on their own roots.

BODY
Spherical body, up to 10 centimetres in diameter, to an elongated-columnar body, growing to 30 centimetres in height. Green to grey-green in colour, with low ribs and short, stiff spination. The crown of older plants is covered in short, reddish brown coloured wool. These cacti do not offset freely.

FLOWERS
Flowers appear in late summer. They are usually yellow, although one or two species have orange-red flowers. Flowers reach 2 to 3 centimetres long. Fruits are red.

PROPAGATION
Usually from seed.

SPECIES
Those seen in collections include *I. bicolor*, *I. copiapoides*, *I. grandiflorens*, *I. krainziana*, *I. maritima FR 590* and *I. paucispina*.

I. grandiflorens

I. unguispina

I. maritima

139

LEPISMIUM Pfeiffer

Subgenus of *Rhipsalis* according to F. Buxbaum

HABITAT
Found over large areas of Brazil, Argentina, Paraguay and Venezuela.

Epiphytic cacti of slender, pendant segments that vary in shape and in the size of their flowers. Typical flower scars on segments are caused by the deeply positioned (sunken) ovary; in all other ways and by their distribution these decorative cacti resemble *Rhipsalis*.

A position of diffused light, a humus-enriched soil mix, and sparse winter watering suit these plants well. They are usually grown in hanging baskets on their own roots.

BODY
Slender segments varying in shape from terete to flat or angular, pendant in habit. Branching freely.

SPINES
Spination is reduced to a few bristles, which are absent from older segments.

FLOWERS
Bell-shaped flowers arise both from the apex and the sides of the segments, depending on the species. White, yellow-white to light red in colour, they open wide to 4–5 centimetres in diameter. Flowering occurs from mid to late summer. The fruit is usually red.

L. cruciforme

PROPAGATION
Propagation is by separating individual segments and planting them in a peat–sand-based soil mix, under conditions of high humidity.

SPECIES
Amongst those found in collections the following are of merit: *L. chrysanthum, L. cruciforme, L. grandiflorum* and *L. marnieranum*.

LEUCHTENBERGIA Hooker

HABITAT
Mexican cacti with a distinctive body shape, formed by triangular tubercles with flexible, long and bristly spines. Older plants develop a thickened stem and offset from the base to form groups.

These cacti are easy to maintain on their own roots. They prefer a coarse soil mix, dry winter rest and a sunny position.

BODY
The body is a simple rosette of triangular tubercles at first; it offsets and develops stems with age. A thick tap root is typical. Greyish green in colour, with off-white to straw coloured, long and flexible spines.

FLOWERS
Yellow funnelform flowers, up to 7 centimetres long, arise from new growth in the apex. Flowering occurs in mid-summer.

PROPAGATION
From offsets or by seed.

SPECIES
A single species has been described, *L. principis*.

L. principis

L. principis (flower detail)

LOBIVIA Britton & Rose

HABITAT

A very large and outstanding group of cacti from Bolivia, central Peru and Argentina.

Possibly the most admired, the most intensively studied and the most widely collected of all cacti, the genus *Lobivia* was superbly described by Walter Rausch in his book, *Lobivia: the day flowering Echinopsidinae*, published by R. Herzig in Vienna (1975).

Lobivia cacti are relatively small plants: some are solitary and become elongated with age, but most offset and form cushions of barrel-shaped, or spherical heads.

The flowers are uniformly funnelform, large but with a short tube (see *Echinopsis*), and open during the day. *Lobivia* flowers achieve an astonishingly great range of colours — every shade of cream and yellow to brilliant red, with all shades in between.

All *Lobivia* cacti grow well on their own roots, although grafting is often used to speed up growth and to increase flowering. This is possibly the most highly recommended cactus for those who wish to start a collection.

All species are hardy, and, with protection from excessive rain, they can be grown outside. They prefer a medium coarse soil mix with full sun and plentiful watering during the growing season. Plants require a dry rest in winter.

BODY

Mostly small and spherical, some solitary and become elongated with age. They form cushions of numerous offsets; all are clearly ribbed and green to greyish green in colour.

SPINES

Spines vary from very short and pectinate (comb-like), to thick and elongated. The spines are often attractively coloured: they can be yellow, brown or red, and the centrals are often longer and dark tipped.

L. famatimensis

L. calineana

L. backebergii

L. densispina (red flower)

L. densispina var. blossfeldii

LOBIVIA

FLOWERS
Plentiful, large and attractively coloured flowers
are funnelform in shape. Some can be up to 10
centimetres long and 6 to 7 centimetres wide.
Buds and flower tubes are hairy; the flowers rise
from the lower mid-section of the body.

Flower colours range from white and yellow to
all shades of red, often with darker centres.
Flowers can be expected from young plants in
early to late summer.

PROPAGATION
Usually from offsets, which can be separated from
older plants at the repotting stage. Seed
propagation is used by larger growers and
nurseries.

SPECIES
A great number of species have been classified;
those listed are among the finest to be found in
collections: *L. akersii*, *L. aurantiaca*,
L. backebergii, *L. boliviensis*, *L. cardenasiana*,
L. culpinensis, *L. famatimensis*, *L. fricii*,
L. hastifera, *L. hystrix*, *L. jajoiana*, *L. multicostata*,
L. neocinnabarina, *L. planiceps*, *L. shaferii*,
L. simplex, *L. tiegeliana*, *L. vanurkiana*, *L. vatteri*,
L. wagneriana and *L. winteriana*.

L. planiceps

L. shaferii

L. silvestrii

L. densispina var. *leucomalla*

L. ferox var. *hastifera*

LOPHOPHORA Coulter

HABITAT
Small spherical and freely offsetting cacti from the southern states of the United States and Mexico; known to natives as *peyotl*, *Lophophora* are said to have magic powers. The intoxicating effect of alkaloid-containing *Lophophora* has been well-known for centuries to Mexican Indians.

These are soft-bodied cacti, with typically a well-developed tap root and felty areoles lacking spination. They can be difficult to maintain on their own roots and in colder climates, so they are often grafted in collections. They can be kept on their own roots if given a coarse soil mix, a warm sunny position and mild wintering.

BODY
Soft, spherical and offsetting to form colonies of small heads. Broadly divided into several low ribs, with typical felty areoles. A thick tap root is also typical. The woolly cover is dense in the crown.

FLOWERS
Small whitish pink or yellow flowers arise in groups from the apex wool in mid-summer. The elongated fruits are red.

PROPAGATION
By separated offsets or by seed.

SPECIES
The best-known species include *L. echinata* and *L. williamsii*.

L. williamsii

L. williamsii

MAMMILLARIA Haworth

HABITAT

The natural distribution of *Mammillaria* extends from the southern states of the United States, through Mexico to Guatemala, Honduras, Venezuela, the West Indies, northern Colombia and Curacao.

With 350 species already named, *Mammillaria* is the largest genus in the Cactaceae family, and there seems little doubt that collectors will discover new species in the years to come.

The name *Mammillaria* is derived from the Latin diminutive of mamma — mamilla (a nipple-shaped organ) — thus giving the more correct name of *Mamillaria*, which is commonly used in some countries (Backeberg, Salm-Dyck and Schumann support this nomenclature).

The uniform characteristic of all *Mammillaria* is tubercles arranged in intersecting spirals, which replace the ribs found in many other types of cactus. A similar arrangement can also be seen in the sub-genera of *Dolicothele* and *Krainzia*, a situation that has resulted in attempts by some collectors to combine these genera under one name.

Mammillaria flowers are small, rising in ring formation from the axils (depressions between the tubercles), and are often accompanied by a ring of wool. The plants are usually small to medium-sized, spherical or elongated and cylindrical, with or without milky sap. The thick or bristly spination is often short and colourful. The smaller species have central spines that are generally hooked, and they also have larger flowers.

A great majority of the species are easy to grow; they are hardy plants that prefer full sun, a medium to coarse soil mix, and a dry winter rest. They often grow well on their own roots, but some of the smaller, soft-bodied species are grafted, as they can easily lose their roots.

BODY

Small or elongated with a spherical to cylindrical shape; habits are both solitary and offsetting. Colours vary from fresh green, through grey to red. Typical of this genus are spirals of intersecting tubercles (mamilla), and a woolly growth in the ring-shaped flowering zone.

M. elongata

M. guelzowiana (Krainzia)

MAMMILLARIA

SPINES
Short, bristle-like and colourful in many species; projecting rigid spines, with longer centrals (which can be hooked) are also seen in the smaller varieties.

In a few species the spination is reduced to a soft, feather-like growth of hair (*M. plumosa*), giving the plants a delicate, thistledown appearance. The colour of the radial spines varies from a whitish yellow to reddish brown; the centrals are often darker tipped.

FLOWERS
Rising from the axils, in rings around the upper part of the body and crown, flowers are small to large, bell-shaped, with a short tube. A woolly growth in the flowering zone is typical of this type of cactus.

Colours range from white, cream, yellow and pink to dark red and mauve, often with a darker stripe. The plants with large flowers (*M. boolii* and others) can be more difficult to maintain, but are well worth cultivating because of the bloom size and colour. Flowering can be expected in young plants from early spring to late summer.

PROPAGATION
On a small scale by offsets or, if being raised in quantity, from seed.

SPECIES
The more attractive species generally seen in collections include: *M. albicoma*, *M. albilanata*, *M. blossfeldiana*, *M. bocasana*, *M. bombycina*, *M. boolii*, *M. camptotricha*, *M. calacantha*, *M. celsiana*, *M. centricirrha*, *M. collinsii*, *M. compressa*, *M. confusa*, *M. dealbata*, *M. diacentra*, *M. discolor*, *M. dixanthocentron*, *M. elegans*, *M. elongata*, *M. fuscata*, *M. guelzowiana*, *M. geminispina*, *M. glassii*, *M. hahniana*, *M. hertrichiana*, *M. ingens*, *M. kraehenbuehlii*, *M. lanata*, *M. louisae*, *M. magnifica*, *M. mainae*, *M. meissneri*, *M. microhelia*, *M. mollendorffiana*, *M. nana*, *M. nejapensis*, *M. perbella*, *M. plumosa*, *M. pringlei*, *M. rhodantha*, *M. ruestii*, *M. saint-pieana*, *M. schiedeana*, *M. spinossima*, *M. supertexta* and *M. wilcoxii*.

M. hahniana var. *giselana*

M. lanata

M. schelhasei

M. matudae

M. magnifica

M. albicoma

MAMMILLARIA

M. bocasana

M. plumosa

M. supertexta

M. longihamata

M. senilis (Mammillopsis)

M. uberiforma (Dolicothele)

M. dioica

M. spinossima var. *sanguiniflora*

M. petrophila

MAMMILLARIA

M. ortiz-rubiona

M. rhodantha

M. bombycina

MATUCANA Britton & Rose

Includes *Submatucana* Backeberg

HABITAT
Peruvian group of cacti of spherical to elongated cylindrical shape, clearly defined low ribs and typically zygomorphic flower and curved perianth. Only some species have hairy flower tubes, so Backeberg has recognised two separate genera.

Coarse soil mix, dry winter rest and sunny position are recommended for all species. They can be grown on their own roots, although they are sometimes grafted to increase the size of young plants.

BODY
The spherical body becomes elongated with age to form a cylindrical shape in some species, clearly divided into low, thin ribs covered with fine spines. Grey-green in colour. Usually solitary habit.

SPINES
Usually short, fine and dense spines, straw coloured to brown. In some species the central spines are longer, darker coloured and can be curved.

FLOWERS
Brightly coloured — flame, orange-red — and have a typically curved shape and long narrow tube. The presence of hair growth on the flower tube is considered important in separating otherwise similar *Matucana* from *Submatucana*. Flowers, which reach 4 to 8 centimetres in length, arise in mid-summer from the apex, showing sparse wool.

PROPAGATION
Usually by seed.

SPECIES
The following species are most popular with collectors: *M. aurantiaca*, *M. breviflora*, *M. calocephala*, *M. crinifera*, *M. elongata*, *M. intertexta FR 693*, *M. haynei*, *M. multicolor*, *M. ritterii*, *M. supertexta FR 690*, and *M. yanganucensis*.

M. aurantiaca

M. madisoniorum

MATUCANA

M. intertexta FR 693 (Ritter)

M. myriacantha

MEDIOLOBIVIA Backeberg

Subgenus of *Rebutia* according to E. Götz

HABITAT
The natural environment of *Mediolobivia* stretches from Bolivia to northern Argentina.

One of the most prolifically flowering groups of cacti, which, because they are small and easy to maintain, have become popular with growers all over the world.

Mediolobivia cacti range from spherical to short-cylindrical plants; they offset to form cushions of individual heads. Spination is colourful and the flowers have brilliant colours and, like *Rebutia* and *Aylostera*, rise from the base of the plant. Some collectors group these three genera under one name, but clearly defined differences in the structure of the flowers exist, supporting the contention that the three genera should be separated (see Backeberg 1976).

The ribs of *Mediolobivia* are formed by thin and slender rows of tubercles, and the flowers have a distinctive ring of wool at the base.

All species are easy to grow and require a medium coarse soil mix, dry winter rest and plentiful watering during the growth period. Grafting can rapidly increase the size of the seedlings, but the plants will grow and flower well on their own roots.

M. schmiedcheniana var. *einsteinii*

M. brachyantha

M. sp. nov. FR 1132 (Ritter)

155

MEDIOLOBIVIA

BODY
Small, spherical to short and cylindrical in shape; greyish green to bronze coloured; and often forming cushions from offsets. The slender ribs are clearly divided to form the tubercles.

SPINES
Bristly, thin and long, usually straight, or interlacing, and dense at the base of the plant. The colour of the spines varies from light brown to darker reddish brown.

FLOWERS
Plentiful flowers occur even in young plants. The flowers rise from hairy buds, which sometimes carry bristly spines. The buds form in a ring shape around the base of each head.

The splendid *Mediolobivia* flowers are funnelform, large and brightly coloured. They range from yellow and white to golden orange and flame red. Flowering can be expected from early to mid-summer.

PROPAGATION
By individual offsets or by seed.

SPECIES
The following are amongst the most attractively flowered cacti; some may be found under *Aylostera* or *Rebutia* names in literature (Rausch and Ritter): *M. albopectinata*, *M. aureiflora*, *M. brachyantha*, *M. brunescens*, *M. elegans*, *M. eos*, *M. FR 1118*, *M. ithyacantha*, *M. pectinata*, *M. pygmaea*, *M. ritterii* and *M. schmiedcheniana*.

M. sp. nov. *FR 1118* (Ritter)

M. ritterii

M. ithyacantha

M. costata

MELOCACTUS Link and Otto

HABITAT
One of the earliest cacti to be imported into Europe was the so-called 'melon-thistle' or 'melanodistel', a species of *Melocactus* from Mexico. It is also found in the West Indies, Honduras, Guatemala, central Peru and northern Brazil.

The cephalium-bearing *Melocactus* are not easy to grow or maintain, and special care must be taken to avoid root loss in older plants, which bear the 'bristly' cephalium crown.

Grafted seedlings grow well in warm glasshouses with higher than usual levels of humidity. Similar growth conditions can be created in an old-fashioned glass garden made from a large jar placed upside-down or an inverted glass fishtank.

Maintaining summer warmth (above 20° C) and high humidity (above 75 per cent) are important. The soil mix should be medium coarse, with an increased humus content and should not be allowed to dry out completely, even in winter.

Because of their sensitive root systems, *Melocactus* plants should either be grafted or cultivated with a minimum of repotting. Older plants bearing the cephalium, instead of being repotted, should be placed in a sufficiently large pot and top dressed with a leaf mulch and nutrients. It is important that plants grown on a glasshouse bench should receive regular misting.

BODY
Spherical at first, the body becomes elongated with age; some species do form offsets. All species form a bristly, cephalium crown from which the flowers rise. The body is formed from a few large ribs, which can be greyish green or bluish green in colour.

The root system is sensitive to repotting and care must be taken, especially with older plants, not to disturb the ball of roots.

SPINES
Thick radial spines with longer centrals which protrude and are slightly bent at the tip. Colours range from tan and yellow to brown or red.

M. rubrispinus FR 1330 (Ritter)

M. canescens

M. ernestii

M. amstutziae

FLOWERS
The small and bell-shaped flowers have a short tube. They rise in a ring formation from the woolly cephalium on the crown. Although small, the flowers are attractively coloured, often in shades of orange and flame red. Plants must reach a mature size before the cephalium is formed; this is usually five to seven years after the seedling stage.

PROPAGATION
Offsets are not formed readily and plants are raised from seed. It is recommended that young plants should be grafted.

SPECIES
The following more attractive species are commonly seen in larger collections:
M. albicephalus, *M. amoenus*, *M. amstutziae*, *M. azureus*, *M. bahiensis*, *M. communis*, *M. ernestii*, *M. macrodiscus*, *M. matanzanus*, *M. melactoides*, *M. peruvianus*, *M. rubrispinus FR 1330*, *M. ruestii* and *M. violaceus*.

MILA Britton & Rose

HABITAT
Short cereoid cacti, freely branching to form low groups, native to Peru. The small, funnelform flowers arise from an apex of mature shoots. Shoots reach 25 to 30 centimetres in length; some species are considerably shorter. These cacti grow well on their own roots if given a coarse soil mix, dry winter rest and sunny position.

BODY
The short cereoid body offsets from the base to form groups. The body has low, fine ribs of green to greyish green colour. Areolar felt is sometimes present.

SPINES
Stout, elongated central spines are present in some species; others have bristly, shorter spination, yellow to brown in colour.

FLOWERS
Small, funnelform flowers arise centrally in the apex of the plants. Flowering will not occur until the plant has reached maturity. Cream to yellow flowers; the fruit is a juicy berry of red colour. Flowers in late summer.

PROPAGATION
By separating offsets or by seed.

SPECIES
Among the better-known *Mila* cacti are *M. albo-areolata*, *M. caespitosa*, *M. densista*, *M. lurinensis* and *M. nealeana*.

M. pugionifera

M. nealeana

MONVILLEA Britton & Rose

HABITAT
A group of climbing cereoid cacti with slender branches and distinctive nocturnal flowers, they come from warm climate, forrested areas in Brazil, Venezuela, Peru, Bolivia, Argentina, Paraguay and Ecuador.

These cacti require a slightly humus-enriched compost that is well-drained. A warm position with diffused light and support for mature branches are also needed. Plentiful watering during summer and dry winter rest are recommended. These cacti are usually grown on their own roots.

BODY
Long, cereoid, slender branches of pale green to white-flecked green colour, more or less prostrate and climbing. The larger species can reach up to 5 metres or more in height. Ribs are low or poorly defined. Fast-growing cacti.

SPINES
Fine, short and bristly. Some species have longer central spines, grey to black in colour, and often bent downward.

FLOWERS
The large, white flowers of funnelform shape are nocturnal. Reaching around 8 to 10 centimetres in length, the flowers arise from the sides of mature shoots after they have reached over a metre in length. Flowers appear from mid to late summer.

M. spegazzinii

PROPAGATION
Not difficult to propagate by green stem cuttings or by seed.

SPECIES
Among the dozen or so described, these are often seen in collections: *M. amazonica*, *M. calliantha*, *M. campinensis*, *M. euchlora*, *M. maritima*, *M. saxicola* and *M. spegazzinii*.

MORAWETZIA Backeberg

Subgenus of *Oreocereus* according to E. Götz

HABITAT
Peruvian cerei from high altitudes, these are
separated from similar *Oreocereus* species on
account of their apical, bristly cephalium, from
which their strongly zygomorphic flowers arise.
Sometimes included within *Borzicactus*
(according to Kimnach), a genus with a similar
flower structure, but without the apical cephalium
growth.
　　These hardy plants are suited to a sunny
position, outdoor culture in frost-free gardens,
and a coarse soil mix. Dry winter rest is needed.

BODY
Short cereoid body, branching to form low-
growing bushes. Well-defined ribs, individual
stems reach up to 1 metre in height. Dark green in
colour.

SPINES
Stout central spines are up to 3 centimetres long;
radials are equally strong. Yellow to reddish
brown in colour. Felty areoles and sparse hair
near the apex are typical.

FLOWERS
The large flowers are up to 10 centimetres long
and 4 centimetres wide, and carmine-red in
colour. The flowers arise in mid to late summer
from the bristly, apical growth (cephalium) and
are strongly zygomorphic.

PROPAGATION
By offsets or by seed.

SPECIES
The following species are amongst the most
attractive: *M. doelziana* and *M. sericata FR 1309*.

Morawetzia sp. (flowering zone)

NEOBUXBAUMIA Backeberg

HABITAT
Originating in Mexico, these cacti are best suited to outdoor gardens in frost-free regions or large glasshouses. Large columnar, tree-like cacti of several metres in height these are relatively easy to maintain, but rare in indoor collections owing to their size. Attractive for their geometrically perfect arrangement of many ribs and colourful dense spination, *Neobuxbaumia* cacti grow well on their own roots in a coarse soil mix, and require a warm position and dry winter rest.

BODY
Tall and columnar, with many ribs, these cacti reach up to 15 metres in height, sometimes branching for some distance above ground. Grey-green in colour.

SPINES
Spreading, needle-like radial spines; the central spines are longer and deeper in colour, upright and dense in the crown. Yellow to reddish brown in colour.

FLOWERS
Cylindrical to funnelform flowers, range from 3 to 7 centimetres in length. In most species they are borne apically, though in some they grow from sides of mature shoots in the upper third of the cactus. The fruit is spiny. Flowering occurs in late summer, after the plant has reached mature height.

PROPAGATION
Usually by seed.

SPECIES
N. mezcalaensis, *N. polylopha*, *N. scoparia* and *N. tetetzo*.

N. polylopha

N. scoparia

NEOCHILENIA Backeberg

Subgenus of *Neoporteria* according to E. Götz

HABITAT
A large genus of Chilean cacti, classified separately from *Neoporteria* and *Horridocactus* (two similar genera) by Backeberg because of their broadly funnelform flowers, which always show recognisable hair growth on the flower tube. The distinction between *Neochilenia* and *Horridocactus* also appears justified on geographical grounds, as the ancient barrier of the Andes comes between the two genera.

Some authors, notably Ritter, argue against the separation, and some of the species named here may, in other books, be listed as *Chileorebutia*, *Neoporteria* and *Horridocactus*.

Full sun, a coarse soil mix and dry winter rest are important for all *Neochilenia*. They are hardy plants, usually small and sometimes even dwarf in size, although a few will reach a greater size and become elongated with age.

They can be grafted to speed up growth, but they will all grow well on their own roots. Typical growth in the smaller species includes tuberculate ribs and hairy flowers and fruits. All the species have woolly areoles and open, funnelform flowers.

BODY
Usually small, spherical and greyish green to dark brown in colour. The ribs are formed by rows of tubercles. The elongated, larger plants have longer, straight ribs.

SPINES
Mostly straight, short and thin, with longer central spines, which are bent up or down. The colours vary from grey to near black.

FLOWERS
Appearing from woolly buds on the crown, the flowers are funnelform. They open fully, and their short tubes are always hairy. Colours range from white and yellow to red. The flowers are medium-sized and attractively set among the longer spines. Flowering occurs from early to mid-summer.

N. napina

PROPAGATION
Mostly from seed as, without grafting, the formation of offsets is not common.

SPECIES
Numerous species have been classified as members of the *Neochilenia* genus by Backeberg. Some of those listed here have been named *Neoporteria* and *Horridocactus* by Ritter and other collectors: *N. atra*, *N. calderana*, *N. chilensis*, *N. dimorpha*, *N. floccosa*, *N. glaucescens*, *N. gracilis*, *N. mitis*, *N. napina*, *N. nigriscoparia*, *N. paucicostata FR 521*, *N. pygmaea*, *N. reichei*, *N. scoparia*, *N. taltalensis* and *N. wagenknechtii*.

N. atra

N. paucicostata FR 521 (Ritter)

NEOLLOYDIA Britton & Rose

Subgenus of *Echinocactus* according to L. Benson

HABITAT
Native to southern parts of the United States as well as Cuba and Mexico, these are small spherical cacti, with characteristically large tubercles; they freely offset and form large groups.

These cacti prefer a warm, sunny position, coarse soil mix, careful summer watering, and dry winter rest. They can be grown on their own roots, though they are often grafted to rapidly increase the size of young plants to flowering size.

BODY
Spherical, low and freely offsetting to form cushions. The body is formed by large tubercles; older plants can be elongated to conical shape. Pale green in colour.

SPINES
The short radial spines are spreading, and dense in the crown. The central spines are often longer, stout and dark coloured; some are hooked.

FLOWERS
The large flowers, which reach 6 to 7 centimetres in diameter, are yellowish green to pink and purple in colour. They rise from the apical region in mid-summer.

PROPAGATION
By separating offsets or by seed.

SPECIES
Among the species often seen in collections the following are common: *N. conoidea*, *N. grandiflora*, *N. odorata* and *N. pilispina*.

N. grandiflora

N. conoidea

NEOPORTERIA Britton & Rose, emended Backeberg

HABITAT
A very uniform group of cacti originating in central to northern Chile, the spherical to slightly elongated (cylindrical) plants bear a characteristic flower with up-turned curving, inner petals. This unvarying and unique flower characteristic separates *Neoporteria* from the similar but geographically distant genera of *Neochilenia* and *Horridocactus*. Some authors unite all three under the one name, *Neoporteria*, and species listed elsewhere in this book (see *Neochilenia*) may be listed in other books as *Neoporteria* (see Ritter, Britton and Rose, Hutchinson).

Neoporteria cacti are attractive plants, with fierce spination and distinctive flowers. A coarse soil mix, dry winter rest and full sun make for successful growing and will ensure that the plants are brought to their best flowering condition.

Well-suited to outdoor culture, *Neoporteria* cacti are hardy and very popular with growers; the lower-growing, spherical types, which tend to flower more freely, are particularly favoured. Seedlings are commonly grafted to bring the young plants more rapidly to a mature, flowering size. Older plants grow well on their own roots.

BODY
Either small and spherical, or short cylindrical and elongated with age. The clearly defined ribs are swollen near the areoles to form chin-like tubercles. The body colours range from greyish green to dark green. Most plants are solitary in habit and do not form offsets.

SPINES
Fierce, and often thick, with noticeably longer central spines, which are darker in colour and turned up or down. In a few species (such as *N. gerocephala*), the spines are reduced to thin and dense bristles, covering the whole body. The colour of the spines varies from tan to brown and near black.

N. litoralis

N. nidus

NEOPORTERIA

N. cephalophora

N. gerocephala

N. heteracantha

N. villosa

N. *microsperma FR 535* (Ritter)

N. *rapifera*

FLOWERS

These are uniform for all species and retain their unique shape, with the inner petals upturned and curving. The flowers are wax-like and glossy, ranging from delicate pink to flame red in colour. Flowering occurs in young plants, especially if they have been grafted. The flower buds are pointed, slender and rise from areoles near the crown. Flowering is from early spring to mid-summer.

PROPAGATION

From offsets formed on grafted plants or, more usually, from seed.

SPECIES

The following are amongst the most attractive species: N. *castanea*, N. *clavata*, N. *gerocephala*, N. *litoralis*, N. *microsperma FR 535*, N. *nidus*, N. *nigrihorrida*, N. *planiceps*, N. *robusta*, N. *sociabilis*, N. *subgibbosa*, N. *villosa* and N. *wagenknechtii*.

NOTOCACTUS (K. Schumann) Berger

HABITAT
Notocactus are found in Argentina, throughout Uruguay, and in southern Brazil.

Attractive and easy-to-grow cacti, which can be seen in most nurseries and collections. They can be successfully grown under most conditions, and flowering is easily achieved, even in young plants. The plants are spherical to oval in shape, with distinctive spination and attractive, large, glossy, yellow flowers.

Optimum growing conditions include a medium coarse soil mix, sunny position and plentiful watering during summer. The young plants flower even when small. Some *Notocactus* species will considerably increase their size and become oval with age, others, which are slow-growing, will remain relatively small. Plants are usually grown on their own roots.

Some of the species may be found listed under the related, subgeneric names of *Malocarpus*, *Eriocactus* or *Brasilicactus* in this book.

BODY
Small, spherical to oval in shape, with numerous, clearly defined ribs. The body colour varies from fresh green to bluish green and reddish brown. Most species have a chin-like swelling around the areoles, from which the spines rise.

SPINES
The spines can be thick at the base and long, with distinctive centrals, or bristly-thin in bright colours. Pale yellow and reddish brown spines are typical of *Notocactus*.

FLOWERS
Large, funnelform flowers rise from the crown. The buds and flower tubes are covered with wool; the flower petals are glossy and are usually yellow in colour. A red-flowering species, *N. uebelmannianus*, is also known. Early to mid-summer is the usual flowering time.

PROPAGATION
Some species offset more readily than others, but they can all be propagated with little difficulty from seed.

N. horstii

N. uebelmannianus

N. allosiphon

N. herterii

N. succineus FR 1399 (Ritter)

N. scopa

SPECIES
N. apricus, *N. buiningii* (subgenus *Malocarpus*),
N. floricomus, *N. haselbergii* (subgenus
Brasilicactus), *N. herterii*, *N. horstii*,
N. leninghausii (subgenus *Eriocactus*),
N. mammulosus, *N. megapotamicus*,
N. muricatus, *N. ottonis*, *N. roseoluteus*,
N. rutilans, *N. scopa*, *N. submammulosus*,
N. tabularis, *N. uebelmannianus* and
N. werdermannianus.

NOTOCACTUS

N. muricatus

N. ottonis var. *ottonis*

N. rutilans

OBREGONIA Frič

Subgenus of *Strombocactus* according to Berger

HABITAT
A monotypic genus of cacti from Mexico, with a characteristic modification of tubercles into thickened, angular scales that form the body.

These cacti can be difficult to maintain in a collection and they are impossible to graft. They require a sunny, warm position, a coarse soil mix, minimal watering in summer, and a dry winter rest.

BODY
The broadly rounded body, to 10 centimetres in diameter, is formed by thickened scales that are bent outward near the apex. Spination is absent, apart from bristles near the crown. These cacti are grey-green in colour.

FLOWERS
The flowers arise from tufts of wool in the crown. The tube is glabrous, large, and opens wide. The white to pale pink flowers, 3 centimetres in diameter, appear in mid-summer.

PROPAGATION
Not offsetting easily, usually by its fine seed.

SPECIES
Only one species has been described, *O. denergii*.

O. denergii

OPUNTIA Miller

HABITAT

The natural distribution of *Opuntia* extends from Canada, the West Indies and the Galapagos Islands to parts of southern Argentina. Some species of *Opuntia* can be found in North Africa, the Mediterranean region of Europe and in Australia as a result of modern introductions.

This is the second largest genus in the Cactaceae family, with species that have a great variety of forms, ranging from the largest tree-like plants (1) to low, prolifically branching species (2), which can be grown in pots or in mini-gardens. Regardless of their size, *Opuntia* cacti always show an abundance of flowers and can have most attractive spines.

Hardy in nature, and often bizarre in shape, the plants are very suitable for outdoor cultivation in gardens or on a verandah. Winter watering should be kept to a minimum, but during summer months, all the larger species benefit from regular watering. It is not necessary to graft *Opuntia* cacti as they will grow and flower equally well on their own roots.

Some *Opuntia* cacti (prickly-pear), bear attractive edible fruits and, in their native habitat, they are collected and sold in the produce markets.

In the past, some nursery-owners have grouped together a number of *Opuntia*-related genera under the same name, but in recent years only those plants with characteristically flat, circular, stem segments have been included in the *Opuntia* genus. Other genera, such as *Cylindropuntia*, *Austrocylindropuntia*, *Nopalea* and *Tephrocactus*, have been classified as distinct genera and sold under their appropriate names.

O. basilaris (front), *O. imbricata* (back)

BODY

Bizarre-shaped body, segmented into flat, circular stems. These cacti vary in size from miniatures to bush-like in size (2) and large trees reaching over 4 metres in height (1). The segments are grey to fresh green in colour, and some separate easily.

O. engelmannii var. *discata*

O. echinocarpa

O. bigelowii

O. fulgida

OPUNTIA

SPINES
White, or coloured in shades of red and brown. Spines can be long and thick at the base, although in most species the spines are short and detach easily. The barbed glochids (hairs or bristles) can be seen on young stems.

FLOWERS
There is often an abundance of flowers, which rise along the perimeter of mature segments. The flowers vary from funnelform to cylindrical in shape and are large and glossy. Colours range from yellow to red, with all shades in between. Fruits are grey-green at first, and red when ripe.

PROPAGATION
Easily propagated by planting individual segments, or by seed.

SPECIES
From among the many *Opuntia* species found in nature the following merit space in a collection: *O. abjecta* (2), *O. aciculata* (1), *O. armata* (2), *O. azurea* (2), *O. basilaris* (2), *O. compressa* (2), *O. ficus-indica* (1), *O. fragilis* (2), *O. galapageia* (1), *O. grandiflora* (1), *O. hystricina* (2), *O. longispina* (2), *O. macrocentra* (2), *O. microdasys* (2), *O. occidentalis* (1), *O. penicilligera* (1), *O. phaeacantha* (1), *O. polyacantha* (2), *O. rhodantha* (2), *O. robusta* (1), *O. stricta* (2), *O. sulphurea* (2), *O. tomentosa* (1), *O. tuna* (2), *O. vulgaris* (1), *O. vulpina* (2) and *O. wilcoxii* (1).

O. engelmannii

O. acanthocarpa var. *coloradoensis*

O. violacea var. *santa-rosa*

OREOCEREUS (Berger) Riccobono

HABITAT
A hardy genus of strongly hairy plants from northern Argentina, Bolivia, southern Peru and Chile. In their native habitat, the woolly growth protects the cacti at higher altitudes from excessive amounts of radiation from the sun (as with *Espostoa*, *Cephalocereus* and similar genera of cactus. The length and amount of wool varies amongst the *Oreocereus* species: sometimes it is short and close to the areoles; at other times it is long and covers most of the body.

Oreocereus plants usually form low groups of slender columns, with distinctive, coloured spines and long, hair-like tufts of wool. Flowering occurs only in older plants; the flowering zone, pseudo-cephalium, is sub-apical (near the crown).

The hollow fruit is yellow-green in colour, and opens at the base to expose the black seeds. This characteristic is unique amongst the *Cereus* genera and was the main reason for classifying *Oreocereus* as a separate genus. However, differences of opinion still exist about this point, and some collectors include *Oreocereus* among other genera, such as *Morawetzia* and *Borzicactus* (Kimnach and others).

Although slow in growth, these cacti are an attractive addition to even the smallest of collections. A coarse soil mix, dry winter rest and a position with full sun will suit these plants well. They grow well on their own roots, but seedlings are often grafted to increase their size more rapidly. The display of colourful spines and woolly growth typical of *Oreocereus* provides a fine background to the smaller, spherical cacti.

BODY
Columnar branches form low groups (1); the taller species reach several metres in height (2), although many are considerably shorter. Ribs are clearly defined and greenish grey. All species have tufts of wool growth in varying lengths. Branching occurs at the base or, very rarely, above the base.

SPINES
Short, radiating spines are white. Long thick central spines project from the wool and vary in colour from yellow to shades of orange and red.

O. hendricksenianus var. *brunispinus*

O. fossulatus

OREOCEREUS

O. neocelsianus

O. trollii

FLOWERS
Flowering occurs from the sub-apical zone, just below the crown; the flower tubes are long and cylindrical with narrow openings. The flowers are cleistogamic, that is, self-fertile, and do not open fully.

The fruits are yellowy green; spherical in shape and open at their base. Colours range from pink to deeper shades of red. Flowering can be expected only in older plants. The flower is close to 8 centimetres long. Flowering occurs in mid to late season.

PROPAGATION
By individual branches, or by stems that can be separated from the base at the repotting stage. In larger nurseries, *Oreocereus* are propagated from seed.

SPECIES
From the handful of species of *Oreocereus* (remembering that some growers may have these listed as *Morawetzia* or under other names), the following are often seen in collections:
O. fossulatus (1), *O. maximus* (2), *O. neocelsianus* (1), *O. trollii* (1), and *O. variicolor* (2).

OROYA Britton & Rose

HABITAT
Large spherical cacti from high altitudes of the Peruvian Andes. They form a uniform group of species with small flowers and short, stout spination.

These cacti are well suited to outdoor culture in regions where dry, frost-free wintering is possible. They grow well on their own roots in a coarse soil mix and if placed in a sunny position. Spination and flowering are greatly improved if they are grown outdoors. A dry winter rest is important. Grafting is used to increase plant size and bring flowering forward. Petals on flowers typically curve inwards.

BODY
Large spherical cacti that become elongated in age, reaching a size of 40 centimetres or more if grown without the restrictions to roots caused by pots. Clearly defined, numerous ribs of fresh green colour. Mostly solitary.

SPINES
Radiating spines are short, stiff and pectinate; central spines are projecting, slightly longer and stout. Yellow to brown in colour.

O. citriflora

O. gibbosa

O. gibbosa

179

OROYA

O. subgibbosa

O. borchersii

O. peruviana

FLOWERS
Borne centrally on crown with typically curving inner petals, small in size, and yellow to pink or red in colour. Flowering occurs in late summer, only after plants have reached mature size.

PROPAGATION
By seed.

SPECIES
Only a handful of species have been described, amongst which are: *O. neoperuviana*, *O. peruviana* and *O. subocculta*.

ORTEGOCACTUS Alexander

Subgenus of *Neolloydia* according to E. Götz

HABITAT
A group of small Mexican cacti that closely resemble genus *Coryphantha*, but they lack the typical furrow on the tubercles and their flowers arise in a ring from the young areoles near the crown. The flower tube is typically hairy.

These cacti grow well, if slowly, on their own roots. They prefer a coarse soil mix, dry winter rest and a sunny position.

BODY
The body is formed of large, rounded tubercles that lack the furrow of *Coryphantha*; greyish green in colour. Individual heads can reach 5 centimetres in diameter.

SPINES
Fine, short radial spines and longer, projecting central spines that are darker in colour and black tipped. Dense spination in the crown.

FLOWERS
Attractive, yellow flowers arise from new axils on the top of the plant, and carry hair growth on flower tube. Flowering will occur on young plants, and is common during mid-summer. The fruit is red.

PROPAGATION
By separating offsets, but usually by seed.

SPECIES
The only naturally occurring species is *O. macdougallii*.

O. macdougallii

O. macdougallii

PARODIA Spegazzini

HABITAT

A large group of globular to elongated cacti from Bolivia, northern Argentina, Paraguay and Brazil.

Most species of *Parodia* are easy to grow; they flower prolifically and present few problems to the majority of growers. They are often grafted to increase flowering, although they grow and flower well on their own roots.

Parodia cacti are attractive, symmetrical cacti, often with a fierce spination, which is yellow or red, straight or hooked. A coarse soil mix and dry winter rest are essential. The best spination and flowering are seen on plants grown outdoors in open-air frames.

With age, many *Parodia* species become elongated, and some growers prefer to maintain the plant's spherical shape by cutting off the head in the spring every seven to ten years and re-establishing it as a new plant.

Apical wool, colourful spines and free flowering are typical features of this interesting cactus genus.

BODY

Fresh green to grey in colour, *Parodia* cacti are spherical to oval in shape. With age, the body becomes thicker and more elongated. Ribs are more or less defined by rows of tubercles. Unless the growing tip is damaged, most species do not offset freely. Short growths of apical wool near the areoles are common.

SPINES

Radiating spines are mostly short and whitish yellow in colour. The centrals are longer and projecting, sometimes straight, but more often hooked or upturned. Radiating spination is dense and interlacing.

FLOWERS

A short flower tube with wool; the brightly coloured flower petals vary from glossy yellow to shades of red and violet. The flowers rise from woolly buds in a ring formation near the crown in mid to late summer.

P. suprema FR 912 (Ritter)

P. maasii var. *rubrispina* forma *P. cristata*

P. maasii forma *cristata*

P. obtusa FR 1125 (Ritter)

P. tredecimcostata FR 739 (Ritter)

PARODIA

P. ocampoi FR 738 (Ritter)

P. maasii var. albescens FR 46d (Ritter)

PROPAGATION
By offsets from damaged mother plants or from seeds.

SPECIES
From the thirty or so named species that occur in nature, the following receive most attention from growers: *P. aureicentra, P. aureispina, P. backebergiana, P. borealis, P. camargensis, P. carminata, P. commutans, P. compressa, P. elegans, P. formosa, P. fulvispina, P. gracilis, P. jujuyana, P. maasii, P. microsperma, P. mutabilis, P. penicillata, P. rubida, P. rubriflora, P. salmonea, P. stuemeri, P. subterranea, P. superba, P. suprema* and *P. yamparaezii.*

P. ayaopayana var. elata FR 746a (Ritter)

P. subterranea FR 731 (Ritter)

P. yamparaezii

P. camargensis FR 86 (Ritter)

P. commutans FR 729 (Ritter)

PARODIA

P. maasii var. suprema

P. tilcarensis

P. maasii var. carminatiflora FR 46c (Ritter)

P. fulvispina FR 727 (Ritter)

PEDIOCACTUS Britton & Rose

HABITAT
A small genus of North American cacti, sometimes united into one genus with *Utahia, Toumeya* (L. Benson) or with *Turbinicarpus* (Marschall). Distribution stretches from the north-west United States, in Washington, Montana and through to Arizona and New Mexico.

Pediocactus are spherical to slightly elongated cacti, which in their native habitat withstand cold, frosty winters. These hardy cacti prefer a coarse soil mix, a sunny position in summer and a cold, dry winter. They are usually grafted in European collections, though they grow well on their own roots elsewhere.

BODY
The spherical to slightly elongated body offsets to form wide cushions of heads. Low ribs are formed by rows of tubercles, grey-green in colour and there is strong pubescence in the crown.

SPINES
Numerous, short radial spines, thin and even bristly. Central spines are hardly different, or only slightly longer and darker coloured. Grey, brown to reddish brown in colour.

FLOWERS
Flowers are borne centrally from the apex. They are 1 to 2 centimetres long and white to pink in colour. The flower tube has tiny scales

PROPAGATION
By separating individual offsets or by seed.

SPECIES
From the handful named, the best-known species are *P. bradyi, P. peeblesianus* and *P. simpsonii.*

P. peeblesianus

P. simpsonii

PELECYPHORA Ehrenberg

HABITAT
Subgenus of *Turbinicarpus* according to E. Götz

HABITAT
Small, spherical cacti from the deserts of Mexico. In their native habitat, these small cacti grow partly buried in the ground.

Depressed tubercles, elongated areoles and pectinate, dense spination are typical. These cacti require a warm, sunny position, careful watering in summer, and a dry winter rest. They grow well on their own roots in a coarse, mineral-based soil mix. Sometimes they are grafted to speed up the growth of young plants and to increase the offsetting of older plants.

BODY
Grows slowly to a spherical then slightly rectangular shape and 6 to 8 centimetre height. Body restriction just above the root system (napiform) is clearly obvious; rows of compressed tubercles and elongated areoles are typical. Grey-green in colour. Older plants offset.

SPINES
Pectinate (comb-like), fine and short spines densely cover the body; white to pale yellow colour.

FLOWERS
Fairly large flowers, up to 2 centimetres in diameter, are bell-shaped and arise centrally. They range from pink to deeper red in colour, and appear in mid-summer.

PROPAGATION
Usually by seed.

SPECIES
P. aselliformis and *P. pseudopectinata*.

P. aselliformis

PERESKIA Miller

HABITAT
A group of leafy, shrubby cactus species from tropical regions of Central America, Florida, Peru, northern Argentina and Paraguay, they are thought to be an evolutionary stage between leafy succulents and cacti that bear spines. They sometimes form woody shrubs with prostrate branches, but some species develop a trunk and reach 6 metres in height.

These cacti are of great interest to cactus collectors apart from their function as rootstock. *Pereskia* stock is best suited to grafting young seedlings. They are easy to propagate, vigorous in growth and, relative to other stocks, small in diameter. These characteristics and their year-round succulence make these cacti ideal stock for small diameter seedlings, though regrafting or re-establishing of older plants after a year or so on *Pereskia* is necessary.

Pereskia cacti grow well in soils enriched with leaf mulch and if well-supplied with water and nutrients during the growing season. Reduced watering during the cooler winter months and diffused light conditions are also important. Green sections of mature shoots will root easily in a sand-based mix in conditions of high humidity; rooting is especially fast if it is assisted by bottom heat.

BODY
Prostrate bush of 1 to 2 metres in height, or tree-like with a woody trunk to 5 to 6 metres high. Vigorous in growth, freely branching. Often used as a rootstock because of the ease of propagation, the small diameter of its shoots, the lack of dense spination and its persisting succulence. Retention of leaves on green shoots is typical. Green to reddish brown in colour.

SPINES
Arise from leaf axils, short or long, from 2 to 9 centimetres long, and sometimes curved. Cream colour to dark brown.

FLOWERS
Small, cup-shaped flowers up to 4 centimetres in diameter; white-greenish, yellow to pink in colour. Flowers are usually clustered in small groups and appear in early to mid-summer.

P. aculeata

PROPAGATION
By short lengths of stems, under conditions of high humidity.

SPECIES
P. aculeata, *P. bahiensis*, *P. moorei*, *P. pititache*, *P. rotundifolia* and *P. vargasii*.

Pereskia is the version of this name originally used by Miller, but more recently this genus has become more widely known in cactus literature as *Peireskia* (cf., Backeberg 1977, 405). Named after a French gardener called Peiresc.

PFEIFFERA Salm-Dyck

HABITAT
Native to Bolivia and northern Argentina, *Pfeiffera* species grow well on their own roots and flower profusely. Small, prostrate or epiphytic cacti, with slender, cereoid stems that branch freely to form groups. Well-suited to hanging baskets, they require a soil enriched with leaf mulch, a position of diffused light, and plentiful watering during the growing season. Dry winter rest and outdoor position during summer increase flowering.

BODY
A cereoid body, with slender stems with few ribs, reaching 40 centimetres in length. Pale to dark green in colour. Offset freely from the base.

SPINES
Thin, short, bristly to needle-like spination. The central spines are hardly distinguishable. Grey-white to yellow colour.

FLOWERS
Small to medium sized flowers, up to 2 centimetres in diameter, usually cream-white in colour. They arise from the sun-exposed flanks of the stems near the apex in mid to late summer. The fruit is a rounded, red berry.

PROPAGATION
Usually by separating individual stems or by seed.

SPECIES
P. ianthothele, *P. mataralensis FR 363* and *P. multigona*.

P. mataralensis FR 363

PILOSOCEREUS Byles and Rowley

HABITAT
A large group of cereus cacti native to many regions of tropical Central America, the West Indies, Mexico, Peru and Brazil.

The numerous species of *Pilosocereus* are amongst the most attractive of all cacti, reaching from less than 1 metre to over 5 metres in height. Their geometrically perfect branches of bluish green colour are crowned by a bristly development of areolar hair near the apex, stout spines and large, glabrous flowers. They grow well on their own roots, though young plants are often grafted to increase their size more rapidly.

These cacti require a free-draining, moderately fertile soil mix, ample moisture during the summer, a warm position, and dry winter rest. They must be protected from low temperatures in winter, but are well-suited to growing outdoors or in large containers indoors.

BODY
Cereoid, stout and branching, from near 1 metre to over 5 metre tall stems. Clearly divided into deep ribs of frosted-blue to blue-green colour.

SPINES
Stout and long, central spines protrude and are up to 10 centimetres long; yellow to reddish brown in colour. All species develop longer, bristly spination in the flowering zone near the apex (that is, a pseudocephalium); some also have more or less developed areolar hair of white colour, mostly in the upper third of the stems.

FLOWERS
Large, always glabrous, and more or less bell-shaped, the flowers are 5 to 12 centimetres long. White, greenish white to pink, and light purple in colour. The flowers of most species arise from the flanks near the apex or, in some cases, from tufts of white wool on the apex itself in mid-summer.

PROPAGATION
Usually from seed.

P. palmerii

P. floccosus

SPECIES
A large number of species have been classified, and the genus deserves greater attention in collections. The following species are most attractive: *P. aurisetus*,, *P. backebergii*, *P. bradei*, *P. chrysacanthus*, *P. floccosus*, *P. glaucescens*, *P. hapalacanthus*, *P. machrisii*, *P. magnificus*, *P. nobilis*, *P. palmerii*, *P. polygonus*, *P. rypicola*, *P. swartzii* and *P. tuberculatus*.

PSEUDOLOBIVIA Backeberg

Subgenus of *Echinopsis* according to E. Götz

HABITAT
The natural environment of *Pseudolobivia* stretches from the Bolivian Highlands to northern parts of Argentina.

It is a group of cacti closely related to *Echinopsis* and the *Lobivia* group and was given a separate classification by Backeberg on the grounds that its flower shape was a natural, intermediate step between the short, day-flowering *Lobivia* and the relatively tall, night-flowering *Echinopsis* (see Backeberg 1976). This view is not uniformly accepted, and many collectors and authors prefer not to recognise an intermediate stage and to list the *Pseudolobivia* species described here as *Lobivia* or *Echinopsis*. Rausch, Ritter, and Britton and Rose, for example, do not acknowledge *Pseudolobivia* as a separate genus. In order to avoid any confusion it should be emphasised that the species listed in this section are those identified by Backeberg as belonging to a separate classification.

A confusion in nomenclature notwithstanding, plants sold as *Pseudolobivia* are well worth growing and are easy to maintain. Spherical to slightly elongated in shape, *Pseudolobivia* plants have large (lobivoid), brightly coloured flowers and spines. A coarse, fertile soil mix, dry wintering and plentiful sun and water in summer will suit these plants well. They are usually grown on their own roots and are recommended to all growers.

BODY
Spherical, medium-sized and fresh green to greyish green in colour. Some species become elongated with age (like *Echinopsis*), others remain spherical, reaching 30 centimetres in diameter. Many do not offset readily unless the growing tip is damaged.

SPINES
Short, straight, radiating spines; in some species the central spines are longer, thick and attractively coloured. One or two species have hooked centrals.

P. aurea

FLOWERS
Long tubes (not as long as *Echinopsis*; longer than *Lobivia*). Brightly coloured flowers of yellow or light to deeper red; a few species have white flowers like *Echinopsis*. In most species the flowers open during the day, but night-flowering species also occur.

The buds rise from depressions on the top of tuberculate ribs near the crown, or apically, and often have a characteristic ring of wool at the base. Flowering takes place in mid to late summer.

PROPAGATION
As many plants do not offset easily, most growers propagate from seed.

SPECIES
From Backeberg's classification the following species of *Pseudolobivia* are of interest (classification according to Rausch is shown in brackets): *P. aurea*, (= *Lobivia*), *P. carmineoflora* (= *Lobivia*), *P. kermesina* (= *Echinopsis*), *P. kratochviliana* (= *Lobivia*), *luteiflora* (= *Lobivia*), *P. orozasana* (= *Echinopsis*), *P. potosina* (= *Lobivia*), *P. rojasii* (= *Echinopsis*) and *P. wilkeae* (= *Lobivia*).

PTEROCACTUS K. Schumann

HABITAT
Small, freely offsetting cacti of elongated spherical to cylindrical stems forming low bushy groups, they are native to Argentina.

Pterocactus species require a coarse soil mix, a warm and sunny position, and careful watering in the summer. Dry winter rest is important. Thickened tap roots and large flowers sunken into stem apex are typical. They can be difficult to maintain on their own roots, so they are often grafted. Grafting also increases flowering.

BODY
Low growing and bushy with elongated stems, 8 to 12 centimetres long. Offset at the base. They are usually grafted because of their sensitive roots.

SPINES
Spines are thin, projecting and up to 3 centimetres long. Central spines are darker tipped, yellow to light brown in colour and often point downward.

FLOWERS
Large, yellow to red in colour, the flowers arise from the apex and have a short tube. They are 4 to 5 centimetres long. Flowering occurs in mid-summer. Sunken fruits are typical.

PROPAGATION
By separating individual stems or by seed.

SPECIES
The following species are seen in collections *P. decipiens*, *P. fischerii*, *P. pumilus*, *P. tuberosus* and *P. skottsbergii*.

P. fischeri

P. tuberosus

193

REBUTIA K. Schumann

HABITAT
A large genus of small, soft-bodied cacti from northern Argentina and Bolivia.

The *Rebutia* cacti are very popular with nurseries and growers alike because of the ease with which they grow and can be propagated, and for their flowers. The numerous flower buds appear during early summer in a ring formation around the plant's base, and it is not uncommon to see a young *Rebutia* with twenty and more flowers at once, each flower twice the size of the whole plant!

Rows of tubercles form the more or less spiralling *Rebutia* ribs, giving the plants a symmetrical appearance. Glabrous scales on the flower tube are typical for all *Rebutia* cacti.

Rebutia cacti are easy to raise, providing their soft body is protected from excessive moisture by a coarse soil mix; they require a dry winter rest and should be watered only during their active growing period. They grow well on their own roots, but they are often grafted to speed up the growth of young seedlings and to bring forward flowering.

In many ways the *Rebutia* genus is similar to the *Sulcorebutia*, *Mediolobivia* and *Aylostera* group (see each genus for descriptions), and *Rebutia* may be sold under any one of these names.

BODY
Small and soft bodies, with symmetrical rows of tubercles forming ribs. The body colour varies from fresh green to darker shades of green. Offsets are formed each year to create cushions of small heads, each bearing flowers.

SPINES
Soft, bristle-like, short and straight spines, with scarcely differentiated centrals. Sometimes interlacing and pointed upwards; dense white-grey spination round the areole is typical.

R. krainziana

R. grandiflora

194

FLOWERS

Flowering is attractive and plentiful, even in year-old plants. Flower buds rise in a typical ring formation from the plant's base. Flowers are funnelform, have short tubes, and are bright in colour. The flower tube has glabrous scales, sometimes very distinct, at other times less so. The flowers are usually slender and mostly flame red or yellow in colour.

Some species are self-fertile and readily form glabrous fruits, which dry out to expose numerous black seeds. Flowering usually takes place from early to mid-summer.

PROPAGATION

Easily propagated by separating the cushions of offsets, or from seed.

SPECIES

From the many species collected in their native habitats, the following have most merit:
R. calliantha, R. chrysacantha, R. glomeriseta, R. graciliflora, R. grandiflora, R. krainziana, R. marsonerii, R. minuscula, R. senilis, R. violaciflora, R. wessneriana and *R. xanthocarpa*.

R. glomeriseta

R. senilis var. *iseliniana*

R. marsonerii

R. vallegrandensis

RHIPSALIDOPSIS Britton & Rose

HABITAT
Epiphytic cacti from Brazil, this genus closely resembles *Epiphyllopsis* apart from *Rhipsalidopsis's* four-angled ovary and fruit.

These cacti grow well on their own roots in a soil enriched with leaf-mulch and in position of diffused light. Ample watering and an outdoor position during the summer months promote increased flowering. Ideal for hanging baskets.

BODY
Segmented, forming low shrubs, clavate in shape and green in colour. Young segments tend toward subterete shape and reddish colour. Bristly hair growth is typical. Branches freely.

FLOWERS
Flowers arise from hardened, apical segments in mid-summer. The small flowers, up to 3 centimetres long, are pink and have a characteristic four-angled ovary. They are regular and bell-shaped. The flower tube is short.

PROPAGATION
By separating segments and rooting these in a coarse soil mix under high humidity, where possible using bottom heat.

SPECIES
Only two species have been described, *R. gaetnerii* and *R. rosea*.

R. gaertnerii

R. rosea

RHIPSALIS Gärtner

HABITAT
A large genus of epiphytic cacti occurring naturally in warm regions of Central America, Florida, Mexico, Argentina and Brazil, as well as in parts of southern Africa, Madagascar and Ceylon. Groups of species of *Rhipsalis* have, at times, been divided into several subgenera, according to the shape of their segments.

These cacti are well suited to hanging baskets and a position of diffused light. Generous summer watering and a soil enriched with leaf mulch, recommended for other subtropical epiphytic cacti, will also prove suitable for *Rhipsalis*. They are usually grown on their own roots.

BODY
Segmented with terete, angular, or even ribbed individual segments, sometimes with bristly hair. More or less hanging or prostrate, some are climbing in habit; offset freely. Some species form aerial roots. Segments are fresh green in colour, and reddish near the tip.

FLOWERS
Small flowers, glabrous with more or less pronounced bristly hair growth at the base of the flower tube. White, greenish yellow, pink to deeper red in colour. Flowering occurs in mid-summer, and the fruits are brightly coloured berries.

PROPAGATION
By individual segments rooted in coarse soil mix and conditions of high humidity.

SPECIES
From the large number of species described, the following are of interest: *R. aculeata*, *R. cassutha*, *R. cereoides*, *R. clavata*, *R. coralloides*, *R. crispata*, *R. cuneata*, *R. elliptica*, *R. fasciculata*, *R. horrida*, *R. lindbergiana*, *R. linearis*, *R. madagascarensis*, *R. pilosa*, *R. prismatica*, *R. ramulosa*, *R. roseana*, *R. shaferi* and *R. sulcata*.

R. hybrid 'China Rose'

Rhipsalis sp.

ROOKSBYA Backeberg

Subgenus of *Neobuxbaumia* according to E. Götz

HABITAT
Tall Mexican cerei that grow to several metres in height and rarely offset. The distinctive bell-shaped flowers are nocturnal, with projecting anthers and sparse bristly hair growth on the flower tube and fruit.

These cacti grow well on their own roots in a coarse soil mix, in a position with full sun. Dry winter rest and, where possible, an outdoor position are preferred.

BODY
Tall, cereoid cacti with clearly defined ribs. Grey-green in colour. Young plants rarely offset.

SPINES
Short, stout and dark coloured. Some central spines point downward.

FLOWERS
Large, bell-shaped flowers can be up to 10 centimetres long, with glabrous scales and sparse bristles on the flower tube. Pink to deeper red in colour, *Rooksbya* flowers are nocturnal, with characteristically protruding anthers. Flowers appear in mid to late summer. The fruit is green.

PROPAGATION
Usually from seed.

SPECIES
Only one species has been fully described, *R. euphorbioides*.

R. euphorbioides

ROSEOCACTUS Berger

Subgenus of *Ariocarpus* according to E. Götz

HABITAT
The natural distribution of this species covers parts of Texas and Mexico. Species of *Roseocactus* were separated from a similar genus, *Ariocarpus*, on account of their centrally borne flowers, which arise from furrow-like depressions on apical tubercles on their woolly crown. The rosette-shaped, flattened tubercles form the familiar body shape of both of these related genera.

These cacti can be difficult to maintain on their own roots. Grafting speeds up the growth of young plants considerably. A coarse, mineral-based soil mix, cautious watering in summer, and dry winter rest are important. A position with warmth and full sun is preferred.

BODY
Rosette of flattened tubercles, depressed-spherical shape; sometimes offsets to form groups of heads that reach 15 centimetres in diameter. Distinctive furrowed tubercles in woolly crown. Napiform roots are typical.

FLOWERS
Flowers arise in early summer from a woolly crown. The relatively large flower, of 4 to 6 centimetres diameter, is pink to deeper violet-red colour.

PROPAGATION
Separating older groups or more usually from seed.

SPECIES
Only four species have been described: *R. fissuratus*, *R. intermedius*, *R. kotschoubeyanus* and *R. lloydii*.

R. fissuratus

R. fissuratus var. lloydii

R. kotschoubeyanus

SELENICEREUS (Berger) Britton & Rose

HABITAT
Vigorously growing, climbing cerei from the warm regions of the southern states of the United States, Central America, Cuba, the West Indies and the north coast of South America.

These cacti are similar in appearance to *Hylocereus*, though the long flower tube and fruits of *Selenicereus* have a distinctive cover of bristly hair or spines. Very large, perfumed flowers open at night, and contain a drug used by the pharmaceutical industry to produce preparations that promote good blood circulation.

Selenicereus cacti require a warm glasshouse atmosphere, with ample moisture and humidity, soils enriched with leaf mulch, and support for their climbing branches. Cool, but not cold, winter rest with reduced watering and a position of diffused light are recommended. They grow well on their own roots.

BODY
Long, slender and low-ribbed stems climb and form aerial roots. Reach several metres in length and are light to dark green in colour.

SPINES
Short bristle-like, usually light coloured spines, but spination is sometimes missing. Hair or spine growth on the flower tube base and fruit are typical.

FLOWERS
Nocturnal and often perfumed flowers are white in colour. The flowers reach 30 to 35 centimetres in length, and have numerous projecting stamens arranged in two series. Fruits are large and red.

PROPAGATION
By cuttings of the stems or by seed.

SPECIES
From the two dozen or so species described, the following are of interest: *S. coniflorus*, *S. grandiflorus*, *S. honourensis*, *S. macdonaldiae*, *S. urbanianus*, *S. vaupelii* and *S. wercklei*.

S. grandiflorus

SETICEREUS Backeberg

Subgenus of *Borzicactus* according to E. Götz

S. icosagonus

HABITAT
Native to Peru and Ecuador. Shrubby to tree-like
cerei. The typical bristly flower zone (cephalium)
and the naked flower and fruit are the two
principal characters in which *Seticereus* and the
similar *Borzicactus* genus differ.

    Seticereus cacti require a position of full sun, a
well-drained, coarse soil mix, and a dry winter
rest. A sheltered outdoor garden in frost-free
regions will suit these hardy cacti well. They grow
well on their own roots.

BODY
Cereoid, with numerous ribs. Reach from 50
centimetres to 2 metres in height, and branch
from the base.

SPINES
Dense bristly to needle-like radial spines of light
colour. Central spines are sometimes stiff, longer,
and dark brown in colour.

FLOWERS
Flowers arise from the bristly *Cephalium* on the
upper third of mature stems. The compressed,
short flower tube is naked, that is free of hair
growth. The flowers are 5 to 8 centimetres long
and red to deep violet-red in colour. Flowering
occurs mid to late summer.

PROPAGATION
Usually by seed.

SPECIES
Four species have so far been described:
S. chlorocarpus, *S. humbolotii*, *S. icosagonus* and
S. roezlii.

SETIECHINOPSIS (Backeberg) de Haas

HABITAT
Short-cylindrical cacti with large, nocturnal flowers originating in Argentina.

Related to genus *Arthrocereus*, *Setiechinopsis* are not difficult to maintain on their own roots in a coarse soil mix and in a sunny position if they are given a dry winter rest and ample watering during the growing season. They are often grafted to increase plant size and frequency of flowering.

BODY
Cylindrical, solitary and up to 20 centimetres in height. Low, numerous ribs with small areoles. Brown-green in colour.

SPINES
Fine, straight and bristly. Short radial spines and slightly longer, darker central spines.

FLOWERS
Large, nocturnal flowers arise from the apex in mid-summer. The long, thin flower tube has bristly scales. Flowers are scented and autogamous, that is, self-fertile.

PROPAGATION
Usually from seed.

SPECIES
Only one species has been described, *S. mirabilis*.

S. mirabilis

S. mirabilis (flower detail)

SOEHRENSIA Backeberg

Subgenus of *Trichocereus* according to
W. Rausch

HABITAT
Stoutly columnar, large cacti, more spherical in
youth, from north-west Argentina and Chile.
   These are high altitude cacti, hardy, and with
typically fierce spination, requiring a position in
full sun, a coarse soil mix and a dry winter rest. In
frost-free regions they can be grown in outdoor
gardens. Usually they are not grafted. The stout
flower tube and profuse areolar hair are typical.

BODY
Large, spherical to elongated cacti that become
columnar with age, they sometimes offset to form
groups. Well-defined ribs, sixteen to thirty in
number, grey-green to dark-green in colour.
Areolar felt or hair is typical of young plants, and
occurs near the crown of mature specimens.

SPINES
Dense, thick and up to several centimetres long,
the brightly coloured spines are in shades of light
to reddish brown.

S. bruchii

S. formosa (red flower)

S. formosa (orange flower)

SOEHRENSIA

S. ingens

S. quebrada

FLOWERS

Funnelform to bell-shaped flowers have a stout flower tube and are bright yellow to red in colour. Flowering occurs from the crown; flowers are 6 to 8 centimetres long. These cacti have to reach considerable maturity before flowering occurs in mid to late summer.

PROPAGATION

Usually by seed.

SPECIES

Several species have been described, and *Soehrensia* deserve greater attention from all collectors: *S. bruchii*, *S. formosa*, *S. grandis*, *S. ingens* and *S. korethroides*.

SOLISIA Britton & Rose

Subgenus of *Mammillaria* according to E. Götz

HABITAT
Small spherical cacti, native to Mexico, with typically flattened tubercles, milky sap and elongated areoles, closely resembling *Pelecyphora*.

Difficult to maintain on their own roots, these cacti are often grafted. Napiform, thickened plant base and appressed spination (that is, spines held close to the body) are typical. These cacti require a coarse soil mix, a warm and sunny position, careful watering during summer, and a dry winter rest.

BODY
Small, slow-growing cacti have a characteristic napiform base and solitary, compressed tubercles and long areoles. The presence of milk sap makes this genus distinct from the similar *Pelecyphora*.

SPINES
Appressed, comb-like, white spines densely cover the green body.

FLOWERS
Arise from the upper third of the body (apically in *Pelecyphora*). The bell-shaped flowers are about 2 centimetres long and yellow-green in colour. Grafted plants flower profusely from early to mid-summer.

PROPAGATION
Usually by seed.

SPECIES
A single species only has been described, *S. pectinata*.

S. pectinata

STROMBOCACTUS Britton & Rose

HABITAT
Solitary, spherical cacti with thickened tap roots and typically four-angled tubercles from Mexico. In its native habitat, the flattened body of *Strombocactus* is partly buried in mineral-rich soil and well camouflaged.

Often grafted to increase growth, offsetting and flowering, these cacti require a position of warmth, full sun, careful watering in summer and dry winter rest. A coarse soil mix with high mineral content is recommended.

BODY
Flattened, spherical body with typical tap root and ribs formed by four-angled tubercles. Rarely offsets.

SPINES
Light-coloured spines are bristly and are absent from older areoles.

FLOWERS
Arising apically, the yellow-white flowers can be up to 3 centimetres in length and diameter. Flowering occurs from early to mid-summer. Very small seed.

PROPAGATION
By seed.

SPECIES
A single species only has been described, *S. disciformis*.

S. disciformis

SULCOREBUTIA Backeberg

HABITAT
A genus* of spherical cacti from north-eastern Bolivia closely related to *Rebutia*. In general growth and flowering they resemble *Rebutia*, but they have thicker spination, a large tap root, and narrow, elongated areoles on the top of tubercles that taper upwards. The free formation of offsets, seen in *Rebutia*, is not so common, although grafted plants form offsets more readily.

Numerous species previously listed as *Rebutia* have been reclassified as *Sulcorebutia* and these, in addition to the new species, have increased to over forty the numbers available.

Popular with growers, *Sulcorebutia* are usually slightly larger than the small *Rebutia*. They have fierce and colourful spines and, like *Rebutia*, flower freely.

A medium coarse soil mix and a position with full sun, combined with a dry, winter rest, suit *Sulcorebutia* well. They can be grown well on their own roots, although they are often grafted to speed up growth and to increase flowering.

S. steinbachii

BODY
Small and spherical in various shades of green and brown. A thick tap root and up-turned tubercles are typical.

SPINES
Borne on characteristically lengthy, linear areoles, *Sulcorebutia* spines are often fierce and long; the central spines are projected and interlacing. Some species carry short, bristly spines with no centrals, or only ones that are scarcely differentiated. The colour of the spines ranges from white and yellow to shades of red and brown.

S. tunariensis

FLOWERS
Simple, large flowers resemble those of a *Rebutia*. Slender and funnelform in shape, the flowers often rise from the lower part of the body. Flowering takes place from early to mid-summer. Colours range from orange and flame red to yellow.

PROPAGATION
Unless grafted, offsets are not formed readily and propagation is often from seed.

S. weingartiana

SULCOREBUTIA

S. hoffmanniana

SPECIES

From the large number of species named to date, the following show merit in cultivation: *S. alba*, *S. breviflora* (previously as *Rebutia brachyantha*), *S. candiae*, *S. crispata*, *S. flavissima* (previously as *Lobivia hoffmanniana*), *S. hoffmanniana*, *S. kruegeri* (previously as *Aylostera kruegeri*), *S. markusii*, *S. mentosa*, *S. muschii*, *S. polymorpha*, *S. steinbachii*, *S. tarabucensis*, *S. taratensis* (previously as *Rebutia taratensis*), *S. tiraquensis*, *S. tunariensis* (previously as *Rebutia tunariensis*), *S. vasqueziana* and *S. weingartiana*.

For a complete revision of this genus and full list of field numbers, see Brinkmann's Sulcorebutia *(1976).*

S. menesesii

S. mentosa FR 945 (Ritter)

S. totorensis

TEPHROCACTUS

Lemaire emended Backeberg

Subgenus of *Opuntia* according to L. Benson

HABITAT
A dwarf *Opuntia*-like cactus from the high altitude regions of Peru, Chile, Bolivia and Argentina. Classified as a subgenus of *Opuntia* by most authors. Numerous species of *Tephrocactus* genus form various intermediate steps in shoot modification from the flattened segments of *Opuntia* to the more rectangular, even angular shoots of *Cylindropuntia* and Backeberg's subgenus *Austrocylindropuntia*. Two major groups of species of subgenus *Tephrocactus* can be divided into sub-groups of globular species and elongated species.

These are hardy cacti, suited to outdoor culture in frost-free regions; they prefer a coarse soil mix, dry winter rest, and sunny position. They grow well on their own roots and branch freely.

BODY
Segmented, freely branching body, to form low groups of stems, more globular or elongated depending on the species. Some high altitude species have a thickened tap root. They are mostly easy to maintain on their own roots, although the smallest species are often grafted. Grey-green, dark green or reddish green in colour.

SPINES
Attractive and variable spination, from long flexible to more stout, with prominent centrals; brightly coloured.

FLOWERS
Similar to all other *Opuntia* cactus flowers, with glabrous ovary and a short tube, opening wide, in bright colours of yellow to red. Flowers range in size from 1 to 4 centimetres in diameter and appear from early to mid-summer. The fruit is a red, fleshy berry of variable size.

PROPAGATION
By individual stem segments in a coarse soil mix, using bottom heat, or by seed.

T. aoracanthus (= *T. articulatus* var. *ovatus*)

T. ovatus

T. rosea

T. articulatus var. *papyracanthus*

SPECIES
From the many species described the following are of interest: *T. alboareolatus*, *T. articulatus*, *T. atroglobosus*, *T. catacanthus*, *T. colorens*, *T. crispicrinitus*, *T. dimorphus*, *T. flexispinus*, *T. floccosus*, *T. glomeratus*, *T. lagopus*, *T. pentlandii*, *T. platyacanthus*, *T. sphaericus*, *T. variiflorus FR 91* and *T. weberi*.

THELOCACTUS (K. Schumann) Britton & Rose

Subgenus of *Echinocactus* according to
L. Benson.

HABITAT
A distinctive group of spherical cacti from Texas
and Mexico.

Moderate in size, *Thelocactus* plants have
colourful, long spines and large, brightly coloured
flowers. They are relatively easy to cultivate in
most positions: a coarse soil mix, a sunny
exposure, and a dry winter rest will suit them
well.

The plants are usually grown on their own roots
and rapidly reach maturity and flowering size.
Tuberculate ribs, with elongated areoles and
scales on the glabrous flower tube are typical.

BODY
The spherical body becomes slightly elongated
with age; greyish green to fresh-green in colour.
The ribs are formed from rows of tubercles, which
are elongated near the flowering zone on the
crown. Some species offset from the base; others
do not.

SPINES
The radiating spines are short, straight, and often
white. The centrals are longer, also straight, but
often coloured brown, red or yellow. In some
species the central spines are flattened and
flexible; most are rigid.

FLOWERS
Large flowers open fully to 10 centimetres in
diameter. They are brightly coloured, in shades of
pink, red or purplish mauve, and often have
darker centres. The flower tubes and buds are
glabrous and carry scales. Flowering occurs in
spring to mid-summer.

PROPAGATION
Usually from seed, though some species offset
readily.

SPECIES
The following species are popular: *T. bicolor*,
T. flavidispinus, *T. heterochromus*,
T. hexaedrophorus, *T. leucacanthus*, *T. nidulans*
and *T. wagnerianus*.

T. wagnerianus

T. leucacanthus. var. *schmollii*

T. bueckii

T. heterochromus

T. nidulans

T. bicolor

THRIXANTHOCEREUS Backeberg

HABITAT
High altitude columnar cacti from the Peruvian Andes. These cacti are slender-stemmed and attractive, with dense spination. Mature plants can reach a height of up to 3 metres; rarely branch. Numerous thin ribs and dense spination are typical for ungrafted plants.

These cacti grow well on their own roots in a coarse soil mix. They require a warm, sunny position, careful watering in summer, and a dry winter rest.

BODY
Slender cereoid and solitary cacti. The stems typically have low, numerous ribs, usually covered by dense spination. Pale green colour. These cacti do not offset easily.

SPINES
Dense, fine, brightly coloured, needle-like spines. Young plants have a characteristic ring of longer bristles at the base; older plants develop areolar wool. Light brown to reddish brown in colour. Central spines are longer, bristly and usually darker tipped.

FLOWERS
Funnelform flowers are large — up to 10 centimetres long — with a hairy tube arising from a bristly cephalium on mature shoots. The colour of flower-tube hair varies from white to brown. Flowering occurs in mid to late summer.

PROPAGATION
Usually by seed.

SPECIES
The most attractive species in collections are
T. blossfeldiorum, *T. cullmannianus* and *T. senilis*.

T. blossfeldiorum

TOUMEYA Britton & Rose

HABITAT
Native to southern parts of the United States.

These small cacti, spherical to elongated with age, and of solitary habit, are difficult to maintain without grafting. Conical tubercles and centrally borne flowers are typical.

A coarse soil mix, careful summer watering, a position of full sun and dry winter rest are all important. Grafted plants offset more readily.

BODY
Slow-growing, the spherical to elongated body can reach up to 10 centimetres in height. Conical tubercles with solitary heads are typical unless cacti are grafted. Grey-green in colour.

SPINES
Flattened, short radial spines, with longer, paper-like central spines, 5 centimetres long and flexible. Yellow-white in colour.

FLOWERS
Bell-shaped flowers are small, up to 2 centimetres long. There are characteristic scales on the flower tube. Flowers arise from the crown in mid to late summer.

PROPAGATION
Usually from seed.

SPECIES
One species has been named, *T. papyracantha*.

T. papyracantha

TRICHOCEREUS (Berger) Riccobono

HABITAT

A large group of columnar cacti, whose natural environment stretches from Ecuador to Central Argentina and Chile. Some species of *Trichocereus* resemble the taller-growing *Echinopsis* in their growth form.

The plants reach a height of several metres (1), or form lower colonies of slender branches (2). The spectacularly large *Trichocereus* flowers are nocturnal, and some remain open the following day as well. The plants are usually grown on their own roots.

Trichocereus are hardy plants, well suited to an outdoor position in a sheltered, sunny corner of a garden. If given full sun, a well-drained, fertile soil and protection from wind, the taller species can enhance even the smallest of gardens.

BODY

Generally tall, columnar branches (1), offsetting at the base. The ribs are clearly defined, with a dark to fresh-green colour. There are also low-growing species, which form colonies of slender branches (2).

SPINES

Vary from short and bristly to thick, long and rigid. The central spines are often longer and darker-tipped. Spine colours range from yellow and brown to dark brown.

FLOWERS

Large, funnelform flowers reach 15 to 25 centimetres in length. The flowers have hairy tubes — slender or thick — opening in the evening and closing during the morning of the following day. Some species flower for longer periods, although this rarely exceeds a day or two. Flowering occurs in mid to late summer. The flower colours range from white and pink to deeper red, and often the flowers are perfumed. The fruits are green, or reddish in colour when ripe, and are generally spherical in shape and covered with hair.

T. cuzcoensis

T. spachianus

T. schickendantzii

T. thelogonus

PROPAGATION
Can be grown from offshoots; from mother plants; from sections of stems; or, in larger nurseries, from seed. Many species (such as *T. spachianus*, *T. pachanoi*, *T. schickendantzii*) are useful as rootstocks for other cacti.

SPECIES
Amongst the more popular species are
T. candicans (2), *T. carmarguensis* (2), *T. cephalomacrostibas* (1), *T. chilensis* (1), *T. fulvilanus* (1), *T. glaucus* (1), *T. grandiflorus* (2), *T. neolamprochlorus* (2), *T. pachanoi* (1), *T. peruvianus* (1), *T. schickendantzii* (2), *T. smrzianus* (2), *T. spachianus* (1) and *T. thelogonus* (1).

TURBINICARPUS (Backeberg) Buxbaum & Backeberg

HABITAT
Small, spherical cacti from Mexico noted for their slow growth, thickened tap root and dwarf stature.

Grafting is often used to increase the size and flowering of young plants, though they will grow well on their own roots if given a coarse soil mix, a warm and sunny position, and dry winter rest. Careful summer watering is essential.

BODY
These dwarf cacti, which reach 3 to 4 centimetres in diameter, have a broadly spherical shape. Ribs are formed by rows of spiralling tubercles, which are sometimes reduced to swelling near the areoles. Dense wool growth in the crown is typical. Body colour ranges from grey-green to light brown-green. A thickened tap root is obvious in several species.

SPINES
Thin, short and downward-curving spines are light cream to brown colour.

FLOWERS
Small flowers, 1 to 3 centimetres in diameter, with a short naked tube with narrow petioles. Coloured from cream, yellow to soft pink colour, sometimes with a darker stripe. Flowering occurs in spring to early summer.

PROPAGATION
Usually from seed.

SPECIES
Among the more popular species the following are of interest: *T. klinkerianus*, *T. lophophoroides*, *T. macrochele*, *T. roseiflorus* and *T. schwarzii*.

T. schmiedickeanus

T. klinkerianus

T. macrochele

T. pseudomacrochele

T. pseudomacrochele (pink flower)

UEBELMANNIA Buining

HABITAT
Spherical to elongated, columnar cacti from the
warm regions of Brazil.

These cacti are rare in collections as older
plants are difficult to maintain on their own roots.
Grafting of seedlings is recommended. They
require a warm position, increased air humidity, a
porous, coarse soil mix, careful summer
watering, and a dry winter rest. A position within
an enclosed, glass growth cabinet, like *Melocacti*,
appears to suit these cacti well.

BODY
Clearly defined ribs on a spherical body that
becomes elongated with age — up to 40
centimetres tall in columnar species. Grey-green
to bluish green colour. Usually solitary.

SPINES
Bristly to more stout spines. The longer centrals
can be curved up or down. In some species the
spines are arranged in a comb-like fashion, that
is, pectinate, or cruciform. Light brown to reddish
brown in colour.

FLOWERS
Funnelform flowers are up to 2 centimetres in
diameter. They arise from a woolly crown in late
summer. Short flower tube and woolly ovary.
Flower colour is uniformly yellow in all species.

PROPAGATION
By seed.

SPECIES
The best-known species in collections are
U. buiningii, *U. flavispina*, *U. gummifera* and
U. pectinifera.

U. pectinifera

WEBERBAUEROCEREUS Backeberg

HABITAT
Native to Peru, the genus *Weberbauerocereus* is closely related to genus *Trichocereus*, though a number of diagnostic characters related to flower structure and flower zone spine modifications suggest that separation of the two genera can be justified.

Cereoid, columnar cacti, tall-shrubby to tree-like and branching at some height, these are hardy cacti, well-suited to an outdoor position in frost-free areas. A coarse soil mix, ample summer watering, a dry winter rest and full-sun position are recommended.

BODY
Cereoid body, tall, reaching several metres in height, branching near the base or further up the stems. Well defined, low ribs, sixteen to twenty in number, and densely placed areoles, especially in the partially modified flowering zone.

SPINES
Fine, needle-like, short radial spines with several stouter central spines, modified in the flower zone to longer bristles. In some species, hair-like growth reaches 5 to 10 centimetres in length. Grey to reddish brown in colour.

FLOWERS
Flowers have a variable structure, ranging from stoutly funnelform to a distinctly S-bend flower-limb. There is strong hair growth at the base. The flowers are yellow-green, white, pink to reddish brown and red in colour, large — up to 12 centimetres long — and, in some species, perfumed. The flowering zone is close to the upper third of mature shoots; flower zone spine modification is typical. Flowering occurs in mid to late summer.

PROPAGATION
By stem cuttings or by seed.

SPECIES
The following species are amongst the most decorative columnar cacti: *W.albus*, *W.horridispinus*, *W.johnsonii FR 570*, *W.rauhii* and *W.weberbaueri*.

W. johnsonii FR 570

WEINGARTIA Werdermann

HABITAT
Small, spherical cacti from eastern Bolivia and Argentina.

These cacti appear to grow more elongated when grafted; a thickened tap root typical. They are hardy plants, known to be amongst the most prolifically flowering of all cacti. *Weingartia* cacti can be grown well on their own roots, or grafted to increase the growth rate of young seedlings. A sunny position, coarse soil mix, dry winter rest and moderate watering in summer are recommended.

Variability in naturally occurring species can make the identification of these cacti under cultivation conditions difficult.

BODY
Solitary of habit, the spherical body becomes elongated in age. Greyish green to deep green in colour. Thick, napiform roots with or without a restriction in the root-neck are typical. Clearly divided, narrow ribs with areolar hair and more or less thickened tubercles. Grafted plants offset more freely.

SPINES
Short, spreading radial spines are light grey to brown; central spines are darker, protruding, stout and up to 5 centimetres long, sometimes curving upward and interlacing near the crown.

W. lanata FR 814 (Ritter)

FLOWERS
Bell-shaped flowers have a short, naked tube, with glabrous scales. Flowers, up to 3 centimetres in diameter, arise from the upper third of the body, sometimes several appear from a single areole. Flowers profusely mid to late summer.

PROPAGATION
Usually from seed.

SPECIES
From the species described, the following are of interest: *W. erinacea*, *W. hediniana*, *W. lanata*, *W. longigibba*, *W. multispina*, *W. neocumingii*, *W. sucrensis* and *W. torotorensis*.

W. erinacea var. *catarirensis*

W. hediniana

W. multispina

WIGGINSIA Porter

Subgenus of *Notocactus* according to E. Götz

HABITAT
Slow-growing spherical cacti, from Brazil,
Uruguay and Argentina, united by Salm Dyck
under the name *Malacocarpus*, many of which
were later reclassified as *Notocactus*, *Wigginsia*,
Islaya, *Pyrrhocactus* and other smaller genera.
Both the names *Malacocarpus* and *Wigginsia* are
used today by growers of species listed here.

These are relatively easy, if slow-growing, cacti
to retain on their own roots. A coarse soil mix,
dry winter rest and ample watering during the
summer months are recommended. Grafting of
young seedlings to speed up their growth and
bring them to flowering is common among
collectors.

W. *corynodes*

BODY
Simple, elongated spherical shape, clearly
divided into low ribs and crowned by a woolly
apex. These cacti do not offset freely.

SPINES
Mostly short, stout and yellow-brown to horn-
coloured spines, projecting or slightly bent
downward. Central spines are larger and
sometimes darker tipped or with distinct banding.

W. *erinacea*

FLOWERS
Arising from the apex wool, flowers are medium
sized, reaching about 5 centimetres in length.
They are yellow in colour and have a hairy tube.
Flowering occurs in mid to late summer.

PROPAGATION
Usually by seed.

SPECIES
From those nowadays retained within this genus,
the following are of general interest:
W. arechavaletai, *W. erinacea*, *W. leucocarpa*,
W. macrocantha, *W. sellowii* and *W. tephracantha*.

WILCOXIA Britton & Rose

HABITAT
Shrubby to prostrate-growing cacti from the southern parts of the United States and Mexico. The cereoid, thinly ribbed stems and spiny, funnelform flowers resemble the related genus *Echinocereus*.

Thin, bristly spines and thickened napiform roots are typical. A coarse soil mix, sunny position and dry winter rest suit these attractive cacti well. Most species grow well on their own roots.

BODY
Slender, soft stems, dwarf in size, reaching 25 centimetres in length. Offsets freely and forms low shrubs or prostrate forms. Numerous ribs of grey-green to bluish green colour. Thickened roots are typical.

SPINES
Fine, thin and bristly or hair-like spines are brown to dark brown in colour. Areolar wool is sometimes obvious. Central spines in some species are longer and protruding.

FLOWERS
Funnelform flowers are large — up to 10 centimetres long and 5 centimetres in diameter — and brightly coloured. They arise from the upper part of the stems or apically. Flowers are white,

W. papillosa

WILCOXIA

W. schmollii var. *nigriseta*

pink or deeper red in colour. The flower tube is characteristically spiny. Flowering occurs in mid-summer.

PROPAGATION
Usually by seed.

SPECIES
A number of attractively flowered species have been described, including *W. albiflora*, *W. poselgeri*, *W. schmollii* and *W. tomentosa*.

W. albiflora

WINTEROCEREUS Backeberg

Includes *Winteria* Ritter
Subgenus of *Hildewintera* according to E. Götz

HABITAT
Epiphytic columnar cacti with moderately stout branches, profusely flowering, and native to Bolivia.

These cacti grow well on their own roots and are well-suited to hanging baskets. A soil enriched with leaf mulch, generous summer watering, and a position of diffused light suit these cacti well. An outdoor position in summer is recommended, and dry winter rest is essential.

BODY
Stout overhanging branches, up to 1 metre long. Clearly defined ribs of fresh green colour. Stems reach 3 centimetres in diameter. Branches freely.

SPINES
Fine, bristly and dense spines of golden yellow colour. Central spines are stronger, protruding and typically elongated in the flowering zone.

FLOWERS
Arising on the sides of the shoots, with a characteristic bent limb, flowers are 5 to 6 centimetres long and 4 centimetres in diameter. Flame red in colour, flowers are plentiful on the sun-exposed sides of shoots. They will remain open for several days. Flowering occurs from early to late summer.

PROPAGATION
Separating individual stems or by seed.

SPECIES
Only one species has been described, *W. aureispinus*.

W. aureispinus

227

ZYGOCACTUS K. Schumann

Includes *Schlumbergera* Lemaire
Subgenus of *Schlumbergera* according to E. Götz

HABITAT

Epiphytic, segmented and freely flowering cactus from Brazil, known also as the 'Christmas' cactus as flowering occurs in December.

Some confusion exists in reference books on cacti as to the relationship of *Zygocactus* with *Epiphyllum* (an old and well-used name meaning 'leafy cactus'), *Schlumbergera*, *Rhipsalis* and other epiphytic cacti that have different segments and flower structure. Backeberg accepted, however, that *Zygocactus* (synonym *Epiphyllum*) has short segments, flowers with long, true-corolla tubes, and lengthy, projecting anthers. The inner series of filaments are united and become a 'short tube' within the base of the flower tube. A typical *Zygocactus* fruit is distinguished by an extremely unusual shape, which can be described as an old-fashioned spinning wheel top, which rests on the remains of the spherical ovary. *Schlumbergera*, on the other hand, is an almost extinct genus, found only in cultivation, not in nature. A number of hybrids of *Zygocactus* and *Schlumbergera*, with a range of flower colours, are also cultivated.

Zygocactus's requirement for a humus-enriched soil mix, usually with peat and leaf mulch added, combines with a need for higher winter temperatures and year-round moisture. An ideal summer position is outdoors, for example, on a shaded verandah or under a tree, in a soil mix that holds moisture and is phosphorus-rich with a low pH value. Hanging baskets are often used with success for *Zygocactus* and other epiphytic cacti. Plants should be brought indoors for flowering and placed in a well-lit position with constant sun and temperature of about 17°C (about 60°F). Watering should be maintained throughout the winter; during summer, pots containing epiphytic cacti can be placed in larger containers partly filled with a mild nutrient solution and water to give optimum moisture and air humidity. Significant changes in exposure to light or temperature — as in a heated room — can result in flower drop. Plants benefit from frequent misting when brought indoors. These cacti are usually grown on their own roots.

Z. Zygocactus × Schlumbergera hybrid (flower detail)

Z. truncatus

BODY
Formed by a series of short, spineless segments that have acute teeth along margin. Grow to form low shrubs with segmented branches reaching 30 centimetres. Colour range is from fresh green to dark green.

SPINES
A few bristles of light colour along the margin and areolar felt.

FLOWERS
The flowers rise apically from mature, hardened segments. The flower has a long, slender tube; the petals curve outwards; and the filaments protrude well outside the flower tube. Flower colour range is pink to shades of carmine red. The flower is 6 to 8 centimetres long and 3 centimetres in diameter. Orange-flowered hybrids with *Schlumbergera* can also be seen in collections.

PROPAGATION
By separation of individual segments that will grow easily on glasshouse hot beds under high humidity.

SPECIES
Only one species has been described,
Z. truncatus.

Z. truncatus (flower detail)

Cactus Societies, Journals and Growers Throughout the World

UNITED STATES OF AMERICA

HENRY SHAW CACTUS SOCIETY

Secretary: Mrs Josephine Coscia
6320 Alamo
St Louis MO 63105 USA

CACTUS & SUCCULENT JOURNAL

Abbey Garden Press
1675 Las Canoas Road
Santa Barbara, CA 93105
USA

Austin Cactus & Succulent Society
President: Bob Barth
602 Terrace Mt Drive
Austin, TX 78746

Cactus & Succulent Society of California, Inc
President: Henry Wagner
547 Eleanor Place
Hayward, CA 94544

Cactus & Succulent Society of Greater Chicago
President: Diane Jursa
7706 N Harlem
Niles, Ill 60648

Cactus & Succulent Society of Hawaii
President: Jim Berdach
1218 Akupa Place
Kailua, HI 96734

Cactus & Succulent Society of Maryland
President: John Flater
731 Brook Wood Road
Baltimore, MD 21229

Cactus & Succulent Society of New Jersey
President: Robert Young
363 Washington Avenue
Rutherford, NJ 07070

Cactus & Succulent Society of San Jose
President: Paul Long
1895 Crinan Drive
San Jose, CA 95112

Cactus & Succulent Society of Tulsa
President: Bill Lyon
139 SE Fenway Place
Bartlesville, OK 74006

California Cactus Growers Association Inc
President: Hans Britsch
1860 Monte Vista Drive
Vista, CA 92083

Carmichael Cactus & Succulent Society
President: Pearl Lemkuil
3808 French Avenue
Sacramento, CA 95821

Cascade Cactus & Succulent Society
President: Michael Foster
2615 NE 137th Street
Seattle, WA 98125

Central Arizona Cactus & Succulent Society
President: Jim Oravetz
13493 N 88th Place
Scottsdale, AZ 85260

Central Arkansas Cactus & Succulent Society
President: Roy James
3500 Bowman Road
Little Rock, AR 72211

Central Ohio Cactus & Succulent Society
President: Malcolm Crotty
1446 W 2nd Avenue
Columbus, OH 43212

Central Oklahoma Cactus & Succulent Society
President: Merril Calvert
11201 Draper Avenue
Choctow, OK 73020

Cincinnati Cactus & Succulent Society
President: John Mascavage
6501 Hamilton Avenue
Cincinnati, OH 45224

Coastal Bend Cactus & Succulent Society
President: Ida Maldonado
1316 Cambridge Drive
Corpus Christi, TX 78415

Connecticut Cactus & Succulent Society
President: Phyllis Phillips
RFD #1 Bx 86 Roger Ft
Lebanon, CT 06249

Cox Arboretum Cactus & Succulent Society
President: Isabelle McDermid
5438 Camelia Place
Dayton, OH 45429

Desert Plant Society of Vancouver
President: Douglas Justice
456 E 45th Avenue
Vancouver, BC V5W 1X4

Fargo-Moorhead Cactus & Succulent Society
President: Fritz Hemm
2101 E Main Street
Fargo, ND 58078

Fresno Cactus & Succulent Society
President: Sue Haffner
3015 Timmy Street
Clovis, CA 93612

Fort Worth Cactus & Succulent Society
President: Nathan Scarber
3403 NW 25th Street
Fort Worth, TX

Gates Cactus & Succulent Society
President: Joe Casey
307 Westwood Lane
Redlands, CA 92373

Henry Shaw Cactus Society
President: Greg Mohn
4050 Shenandoah Street
St Louis, MO 63110

Houston Cactus & Succulent Society
President: Hank E. Andresen
8822 Bobwhite Drive
Houston, TX 77074

Indiana Cactus & Succulent Society
President: Charles Miller
4380 W 1200 N-90 Street
Roanoke, IN 46783

Kansas City Cactus & Succulent Society
President: Jack Makepeace
7109 Riggs Street
Overland Park, KS 66204

Las Vegas Cactus & Succulent Society
President: Walter Bzlke
3814 Pecan Lane
Las Vegas, NV 89115

Lincoln Cactus & Succulent Society
President: Daniel Rhoads
2755 Pear Street
Lincoln, NE

Long Beach Cactus Club
President: Rowena Thompson
1303 Broad Avenue
Wilmington, CA 90744

Long Island Cactus & Succulent Society
President: Jack Friedman
5046 Clearview Expwy
New York, NY 11364

Los Angeles Cactus & Succulent Society
President: Chas Spotts
21129 Merridy Street
Chatsworth, CA 91311

Louisiana Cactus & Succulent Society
President: Beverly Siemssen
106 Aster Lane
Waggaman, LA 70094

Memphis Cactus Society
President: Steve Carpenter
84 N Evergreen #11
Memphis, TN 38104

Michigan Cactus & Succulent Society
President: Patricia Dean
3921 Auburn Drive
Royal Oak, MI 48072

Mid-Iowa Cactus & Succulent Society
President: Loraine Eldridge
1430 25th Street
Des Moines, IA 50311

Monterey Bay Area Cactus & Succulent Society
President: Naomi Bloss
134 Trabing Road
Watsonville, CA 95076

National Capital Cactus & Succulent Society
President: Al Nichols
1619 Millersville Road
Millersville, MD 21108

New Mexico Cactus & Succulent Society
President: C. V. Porter
423 13th NW Street
Albuquerque, NM 87102

North Texas Cactus & Succulent Society
President: Harold Messmore
4128 Hackmore Loop
Irving, TX 75061

Omaha Cactus & Succulent Society
President: Sue Steward
12618 Orchard Street
Omaha, NE 68137

Oregon Cactus & Succulent Society
President: Bill Beaston
16038-A S W Reese Road
Lake Oswego, OR 97035

Palomar Cactus & Succulent Society, Inc
President: Reese Brown
2711 Athens Avenue
Carlsbad, CA 92008

Peninsula Succulent Club
President: Eleanor Koch
848 Miramar Terrace
Bohmont, CA 94002

Philadelphia Cactus & Succulent Society
President: Hans Zutter
83 Belair Road
Warminster, PA 18974

Redwood Empire Cactus & Succulent
Society
President: Carol Hill
350 4th Street
Lakeport, CA 95453

Sacramento Cactus & Succulent Society
President: Ron Burnight
3836 65th Street
Sacramento, CA 95820

San Antonio Cactus & Xerophyte Society
President: Gene Turpin
230 Killarney Drive
San Antonio, TX 78223

San Gabriel Valley Cactus & Succulent
Society
President: Joe Clements
14731 La Forge Street
Whittier, CA 90603

South Bay Epiphyllum Society
President: Dick Kohlschreiber
1801 W 27th Street
San Pedro, CA 90732

Stockton Cactus & Succulent Society
President: Keith Wilcox
519 Milo Road
Modesto, CA 95350

Sunset Succulent Society Inc
President: Rosalie Gorchoft
954 S Barrington Avenue
Los Angeles, CA 90049

Texas Association of Cactus & Succulent
Society
President: Mary Jo Gussett
11807 Dover Street
Houston, TX 77031

Toronto Cactus & Succulent Club
President: David Naylor
RR 2
Georgetown, Ont L7G 4S5

Wasatch Cactus & Succulent Society
President: Bart Gallagher
3234 S 800 East Street
Salt Lake City, UT 84106

Wisconsin Cactus & Succulent Society
President: Roland Steinle, Jr
1962 N Prospect Drive
Greendale, WI 53129

UNITED KINGDOM

NATIONAL CACTUS & SUCCULENT SOCIETY

Secretary: Miss W. E. Dunn
43 Dewar Drive
Sheffield, 57 2GR
England

JOURNAL OF THE CACTUS & SUCCULENT SOCIETY OF GREAT BRITAIN

Secretary: 67 Gloucester Court
Kew Road
Richmond, Surrey TW9 3EA
England

BRADLEYA, the BCSS yearbook

Editors: N. P. Taylor
The Herbarium
Royal Botanical Gardens, Kew
Richmond, Surrey TW9 3AE
England
                    C.C. Walker
Dept of Biology
Open University
Milton Keynes, Bucks MK7 6AA
England

ZONAL REPRESENTATIVES

Zone 1 Darlington, Northumbria, Teesside
Mr R. E. Pounder
15 Dryburn Road
Durham DH1 5AJ
Tel. 091-386 1768

Zone 2 Barrow and District, Fylde Coast,
Lancaster, North Fylde, West Cumbria
(Whitehaven)
Mr R. R. Hewitt
16 Belle Vue Drive
Lancaster LA1 4DE
Tel. Lancaster (0524) 66300

Zone 3 Barnsley, Bradford, Bridlington,
Horbury and District, Huddersfield, Hull,
Leeds, Scarborough, Sheffield, York
Mr D. V. Slade
15 Brentwood Crescent
Hull Road, York YO1 5HU
Tel. York (0904) 410512

Zone 4 Derby, Doncaster and District,
Grimsby, Lincoln, Nottingham, Scunthorpe
Mr A. Johnston
11 Malvern Road
Scunthorpe, S. Humberside DN17 1EL
Tel. Scunthorpe (0724) 841503

Zone 5 Chester and District, Heswall,
Liverpool, Mid-Cheshire, Southport,
Warrington

Mr M. Roberts
20 Beta Close
New Ferry, Wirral, Merseyside L62 5BY
Tel. 051-645 4849

Zone 6 Bedford and District, Berkhamsted
and District, Cambridge and District,
Coventry and District, Harrow-on-the-Hill,
Kettering, Leicester, Luton,
Northamptonshire
Mr R. W. Sims
21 Nathaniel Walk
Tring, Herts HP23 5DQ
Tel. Tring (044-282) 2669

Zone 7 Lowestoft, Norwich, Peterborough,
Spalding, Thetford
Mr T. Jenkins
St Catherine's Lodge
Cranesgate Road
Whaplode St Catherines
Nr Spalding, Lincs PE12 6SR
Tel. Holbeach St Johns (040-634) 373

Zone 8 Birmingham and District, Oxford,
Shrewsbury
Mr G. Wheeler
9 Little London Green
Oakley, Aylesbury, Bucks HP18 9QL
Tel. Brill (0844) 237378

Zone 9 Bristol, Cardiff, Gloucester, North
Wilts, Swindon
Ms S. Barker-Fricker
Southwest View House
49 Shoscombe
Bath, Avon BA2 8LS
Tel. Radstock (0761) 32566

Zone 10 Barnstaple, Bridgwater, Cornwall,
Exeter, Plymouth, Yeovil and District
Mr P. Goodson
5 Granary Lane
Budleigh Salterton, Devon EX9 6ES
Tel. Budleigh Salterton (039-54) 5432

Zone 11 Isle of Wight, New Forest,
Portsmouth, Southampton
Mr D. J. Phillips
27 Mountfield Road
Hythe, Southampton, Hants SO4 4AQ
Tel. Hythe (0703) 843266

Zone 12 Brighton and Hove, Chichester,
Crawley, Haywards Heath and District,
Littlehampton, Worthing
Dr A. W. Mace
12 Mill Rise
Brighton, Sussex BN1 5GD
Tel. Brighton (0273) 509171

Zone 13 Farnborough, Guildford and
Godalming, Kingston-on-Thames and
District, Reading and Basingstoke, Walton
and Hersham, Woking
Mr J. Bishop
12 Arbour Close
Fetcham, Leatherhead, Surrey KT22 9DZ
Tel. Leatherhead (0372) 378021

Zone 14 Ashford and District, Bromley,
Croydon, Dartford, Dover, Edenbridge,
Eltham, Herne Bay, Isle of Sheppey,
Medway Towns, North Surrey, Tonbridge
Dr P. Lewis
39 Broadhurst Drive
Kennington, Ashford, Kent TN24 9RQ
Tel. Ashford (0233) 33248

Zone 15 Chelmsford, Clacton-on-Sea, Enfield, Essex (Ilford), Harlow, Havering, Ipswich, North London, Rayleigh, Southend-on-Sea and District, Waltham Forest
Mr E. A. Harris
49 Chestnut Glen
Hornchurch, Essex RM12 4HL
Tel. Hornchurch (040-24) 47778

Zone 17 Northern Ireland
Mr C. C. Baxter
18 Sydenham Avenue
Belfast BT4 2DR
Tel. Belfast (0232) 659636

Zone 18 Ayr, Edinburgh, Fife, Glasgow, Grampian (N.E. Scotland)
Mrs C. Muir
2 Mellerstain Road
Kirkcaldy, Fife KY2 6UA
Tel. Kirkcaldy (0592) 267920

Zone 19 Macclesfield and East Cheshire, Manchester, Stoke-on-Trent
Mr P. Bint
313 Manchester New Road
Alkrington, Middleton, Manchester M24 1NR
For telephone number (ex-directory) please contact hon. BCSS secretary.

GERMANY

KAKTEEN UND ANDERE SUKKULENTEN (in German)

Editor: Mr Dieter Honig
Ahornweg 9, D-7820 Titisee
Neustadt West Germany

DEUTSCHE KAKTEEN (in German)

Editor: Gesselshaft e.V. Moorkamp
22 D-3008 Garbsen 5,
West Germany

AUSTRALIA

SPINE

Journal of Australian Society of Cacti & Succulents
Secretary: Mrs J. Tonoli
53 Manningtree Road
Hawthorn Victoria 3122

CACTUS & SUCCULENT

Journal of Cactus & Succulent Society of New South Wales
Secretary: Mr I. Harvey
32 High Street
Woonona NSW 2517

SUCCULENT PUBLICATIONS OF SOUTH AUSTRALIA INC.

PO Box 572
Gawler SA 5118

AUSTRALIAN CACTUS & SUCCULENT ASSOCIATION

Coordinator ACSA
Mrs Lyn Schultz
Jolly's Road
Teesdale Victoria 3328

CACTUS & SUCCULENT SOCIETY OF THE ACT

GPO Box 2499
Civic ACT 2600

CACTUS & SUCCULENT SOCIETY OF NEW SOUTH WALES INC.

PO Box 36
Woollahra NSW 2025

CENTRAL COAST CACTUS & SUCCULENT CLUB OF NSW INC.

10 Blackford Avenue
Kanwal NSW 2559

EPIPHYTIC CACTI– ASCLEPIADACEAE SOCIETY OF AUSTRALIA

32 Wynyard Street
Rossmore NSW 2171

GOULBURN CACTUS & SUCCULENT GROUP

1 Little Addison Street
Goulburn NSW 2580

MURRAY REGION CACTUS & SUCCULENT CLUB INC.

102 Thomas Mitchell Drive
Wodonga Victoria 3690

SUMMERLAND CACTUS & SUCCULENT SOCIETY

37 Laurel Avenue
Casino NSW 2470

WESTERN SUBURBS CACTUS CLUB

16 Paterson Crescent
Fairfield NSW 2165

CENTRAL QUEENSLAND SUCCULENT SOCIETY

PO Box 6407
North Rockhampton
Queensland 4701

QUEENSLAND SUCCULENT SOCIETY

PO Box 65
Fortitude Valley Queensland 4006

FAR NORTH QUEENSLAND SUCCULENT SOCIETY

17 Suhle Street
Edmonton Queensland 4869

CACTUS & SUCCULENT SOCIETY OF SOUTH AUSTRALIA INC.

PO Box 37
Rundle Mall SA 5000

CACTUS & SUCCULENT SOCIETY OF SOUTH AUSTRALIA INC.

SE BRANCH, MT GAMBIER
Attamurra Cottage,
Attamurra Road
Mount Gambier SA 5290

SOUTHERN TASMANIA CACTUS & SUCCULENT CLUB

1 Willow Walk
Austin's Ferry Tasmania 7011

BALLARAT CACTUS & SUCCULENT SOCIETY

8 Margaret Street
Wendouree Victoria 3355

CACTUS & SUCCULENT SOCIETY OF AUSTRALIA INC.

19 Kingsley Street
Camberwell Victoria 3124

GEELONG CACTUS & SUCCULENT CLUB INC.

c/o Mr J. Edmonds
Torquay Road
Mount Duneed Victoria 3126

SUNRASIA CACTUS & SUCCULENT SOCIETY

PO Box 1475
Mildura Victoria 3500

BUNBURY CACTUS & SUCCULENT STUDY GROUP

Lot 100 Bridge Street
Boyanup WA 6237

CACTUS & SUCCULENT SOCIETY OF WESTERN AUSTRALIA INC.

384 Hardy Road
Cloverdale WA 6105

EPIPHYTIC CACTI & HOYA SOCIETY OF AUSTRALIA

PO Box 210
Morley WA 6062

W.A. CACTUS & OTHER SUCCULENT STUDY GROUP

17 Parramata Road
Doubleview WA 6018

NEW ZEALAND

NEW ZEALAND CACTUS & SUCCULENT SOCIETY
JOURNAL

Dominion Secretary: Mrs A. B. Carlton
164 Massey Street
Frankton, Hamilton
New Zealand

NEW ZEALAND CACTUS & SUCCULENT SOCIETY BRANCHES

Auckland
Secretary: Mr H. S. Norrie
2 Erima Avenue
Point England, Auckland 6
Tel. 572-315

Balclutha
Secretary: Mrs A. Coutts
PO Box 58
Balclutha
Tel. 81-517

Bay of Plenty
Secretary: Mrs M. Galbreath
22 Gilmore Street
Te Puke

Christchurch
Secretary: Mr T. Brownlee
7 Cavan Place
Christchurch 5
Tel. 851-298

Foxton
Secretary: Mr M. Capenerhurst
36 Broadhead Avenue
Wanganui

Hamilton
Secretary: Mrs A. B. Carlton
164 Massey Street
Frankton, Hamilton
Tel. 76-240

Hawkes Bay
Mrs M. Bluck
43 Murphy Road
Taradale, Napier
Tel. 44-7412

Invercargill
Secretary: Mr J. Rogers
259 Queens Drive
Invercargill
Tel. 79-404

Levin
Secretary: Mrs S. Beisel
4 Dunbar Street
Levin

New Plymouth
Secretary: Mrs A. Moratti
39 Maire Street
Inglewood

Northland
Secretary: Mrs L. Jankins

6 Wallace Street
Whangarei
Tel. 487-872

Palmerston North
Secretary: Mrs E. Olsen
42 Tyne Street
Palmerston North

Papakura
Secretary: Mrs M. Williams
2 Beach Road
Papakura

Paramount Dunedin
Secretary: Miss L. Kimmond
10 Lochend Street
Tainui, Dunedin
Tel. 44-941

South Taranaki
Secretary: Mrs B. Cleland
Gordon Road, RD 22
Stratford
Tel. (0663) 744

Wellington & Hutt Valley
Secretary: Mr E. Verrity
65 Harbour View Road
Northland, Wellington
Tel. 759-421

Central Taranaki
Secretary: Mrs J. H. Anglesey
6 London Street
Eltham

Christchurch Cactus & Succulent Society
Journal: *Cactochat*
Secretary: Mr L. McCausland
79 Creyke Road
Christchurch 4

Selected Suppliers of Cactus and Succulent Plants and Seeds

UNITED STATES OF AMERICA

B & B Cactus Farm
11550 East Speedway
Tucson, Arizona 85748

Bach's Cactus Nursery
8602 North Thornydale Road
Tucson, Arizona 85741

Tanque Verde Greenhouses
10810 East Tanque Verde Road
Tucson, Arizona 85749

Burks Nursery
PO Box 1207
Benton, Arkansas, 72015-1207

Abbey Garden
Cactus and Succulent Nursery
4620 Carpinteria Avenue
Carpinteria, California 93013

Cactus by Mueller
10411 Rosedale Hwy.
Bakersfield, California 93308

Cactus Unlimited
Gardena Drive
Cupertino, California 95014

Cycadia
17337 Chase Street
Northridge, California 91325

Fernwood Plants
PO Box 268
Topanga, California 90290

Grigsby Cactus Gardens
2326 & 2354 Bella Vista
Vista, California 92083

Henrietta's Nursery
1345 North Brawley
Fresno, California 93711

Kimura International, Inc.
18435 Rea Avenue
PO Box 327
Aromas, California 95004

Mr Kirkpatricks
27785 De Anza Street
Barstows, California 92311

Singer's Growing Things
17806 Plummer Street
Northridge, California 91325

Crump Greenhouse
Box 185
225 S. Pleasant Ave
Buena Vista, Colorado 81211

Florida Cactus, Inc.
PO Drawer D
Apopka, Florida 32703

Drummong Nursery & Greenhouse
Route 1, Long Road
De Soto, Missouri 63020

Mesa Garden
PO Box 72
Belen, New Mexico 87002

Desert Dan's
Nursery Seed Company
Minotola, New Jersey 08341

Oakhill Gardens
1960 B Cherry Knoll Road
Dallas, Oregon 97338

Redlo Cacti, Inc.
2315 NW Circle Blvd
Corvallis, Oregon 97330

R & J Cactus
12315 Lynda Drive
Houston, Texas 77038

UNITED KINGDOM

Southwest Seeds Ltd
200 Spring Road
Kempston, Bedford MK42 8ND
England

Mrs D. Pritchard
11 Shaftesbury Avenue
Penketh, Warrington, Cheshire WA5 2DP
England

GERMANY

Bisnaga Kakteen-Kulturen
D 6749, Steinfeld, BRD

Piltz, Monschauer
Landstrasse 162 D 5160, Dueren-Bigel,
BRD

Max Schleipfer
Sedlweg., D 8902 Neusaes bei Augsburg,
BRD

K. Uhlig
Lilienstrasse 5, D 7053 Kernen,
Rommelshausen, BRD

Mr G. Koehres
Bahnstrasse 101,D-6106
Erzhousen, Darmstadt, West Germany

Mr V. Thiele
D-6200 Erbenheim, Wiesbaden,
Rennibahnstrasse 8, West Germany

HOLLAND

Hovens Cactuskwekerij
Lottum, Netherland

Fam. van Donkelaar
Werkendam, Netherland

BELGIUM

Gebr. De Herdt
Schommeweg 3
B-2310 Rijevorsel

NEW ZEALAND

New Zealand Cactus Co. Ltd
Chaplin Street
Mangere East, Auckland
PO Box 63-100, Papatoetoe South

Palmer's Garden Centre branches
Great North Road
Glen Eden, Auckland

580 Hillsborough Road
Lynfield, Auckland

120 Pakuranga Road
Pakuranga, Auckland

36A Coronation Street
Mangere, Auckland

Planters World Garden Centre
High Street
Lower Hutt

Oderings Nursery Christchurch Ltd
92 Stourbridge Street
Spreydon, Christchurch

McNab's Epiphyllum Nursery
PO Box 3070 Onerahi
Whangarei, Northland

AUSTRALIA

Australian Cactus and Succulent Supplies
(Geoff Barker)
Lot 3, Cessnock Road
Sunshine, NSW 2263

Arizona Cacti Nursery (John Dixon)
RMB 111 Windsor Road
Box Hill, NSW 2765

Hamilton's World of Cacti
Lot 2, 4th Avenue
Llandilo, NSW 2760

Mrs Joscelyn Burnett
'Andoran'
Darkes Forest, NSW 2508

Buena Vista Nursery (Des Ellery)
Wynyard Avenue
Rossmore, NSW 2171

John Spencer
1 Little Addison Street
Goulburn, NSW 2580

Orana & Mexicana Cacti and Succulent
Gardens (Lester Meyers)
57 Wamboin Street
Gilgandra, NSW 2827

Sunshine Coast Cactus Nursery (Brendon Barker)
5 Daniel Street
Nambour, Qld 4560

R. & C. Metcalfe
Crittenden Road
Glasshouse Mountains, Qld 4518

Cacti Collectors Corner
Garden World Nurseries (Tom Kapitany)
Spring Vale Road
Keysborough, Vic. 3173

Tarrington Exotics (Rudolph Schulz)
Jolly's Road
Teesdale, Vic. 3328

R. Field
'Whiora'
Tennyson, Vic. 3572

McGrath's Cacti Nursery (Roy and Veronica McGrath)
Lot 102, Canning Vale
Perth, WA 6155

Cactus Jim (John Rawlings)
137 Eudoria Street
Gosnells, WA 6110

EPI Centre of Australia
PO Box 223
York, WA 6302

Cactus Desert Nursery
Mypolonga, SA 5254

Aridaria
PO Box 967
Gawler, SA 5118

GLOSSARY OF TECHNICAL TERMS

ACARIASIS   Infection by mites.

ACICULAR   Slender needle-like body, needle-like spines or bristles.

ACUTE   Sharp at the end, coming to a point.

ANOMALOUS   Non-conforming, deviating from the usual.

ANTHER   The pollen sac carried on the top of each filament.

APEX   The upper side of the tubercle from which the flowers or wool arise.

APICULATE   Ending in a short and sharp tip, having a minute apex.

APPRESSED   Flattened against another part of the plant as in spine; held closely.

AREOLE(S)   In cacti, the specialised area from which the spines, wool or flowers rise; the cell nucleus of the plant.

ARTICULATE   Jointed or having a node (joint).

ASCENDING   Curling upwards, as in spines or flower petals.

ASSIMILATION   A process of plant metabolism by which simple sugars (assimilates) are produced in the green parts of a plant — such as the leaf or stem — which contain chlorophyll. Sunlight (energy), carbon dioxide (from the atmosphere) and moisture (supplied by the roots) are all required for this.

ASYMMETRICAL   Lacking regular shape, with parts not arranged correspondingly.

AXIL   Where the upper side of the leaf joins the stem or tubercle.

BANDED   Marked with stripes of colour.

BRACT   A flattened scale-like appendage to another organ.

BERRY   A simple fruit with fleshy pericarp (seed-vessel).

BINOMINAL NOMENCLATURE   A system of botanical nomenclature introduced by Linnaeus (1707–1778). Plant names are classified by a minimum of two words — the generic name and the name(s) of the species.

BRISTLE   Stiff hair or very fine, soft flexible spine.

CALCAREOUS   Chalky, rich in lime; usually a soil type with an alkaline reaction (above pH7).

CESPITOSE   Growing in tufts or clumps.

CALLUS   A hardened plant tissue that forms over a wound or cut.

CALYX   The outer ring of the parts of a flower, a floral tube or cup.

CAMPANULATE   Bell-shaped.

CAPSULE   A dry, dehiscent seed vessel composed of two or more parts (carpels).

CARPEL   Pistil-cell, whether pistil is one cell or several. The modified leaf in which are produced the ovules, the individual constructive, physiological units of the plant body.

CENTRAL SPINE(S)   The spine(s) rising from the centre of the areole, usually protruding and distinct from an outer ring; they are longer or coloured in most cacti.

CEPHALIUM   Woolly or bristly growth of the flowering zone formed by elongation of spines and areolar hair. Compression of growth within the cephalium zone causes its dense appearance. The occurrence of a true cephalium or pseudocephalium is recognised as a marker characteristic by some botanists. True cephalium is said to arise from a deep cleft, such as in *Espostoa*, whilst pseudocephalium is simply formed by spine or bristle elongation, as in *Pseudoespostoa*, without the deep cleft.

CEREOID   Columnar body shape of all cereus-like cacti.

CHLOROPHYLL   The green pigment in plants. Essential for photosynthesis.

CLAVATE   Club-shaped body form of older cacti.

CLEISTOGAMOUS   Pollination and fertilisation take place in an unopened flower.

COLUMNARIUS   Of the nature or form of a column, columnar.

COMPRESSED   Flattened shape.

COROLLA   The inner ring of the parts of a flower consisting of the petals, usually brightly coloured.

COTYLEDON   A seed leaf, forming part of the embryo of a seed. The first leaf to develop when a seed germinates (dicotyledonous — possessing two cotyledons).

CRISTATUS (CRISTATE)   Crested, forming a fasciated condition, compressed and massed together (relates to shape).

CRUCIFORM   Shaped like a cross.

CUTTING   A vegetative part of the plant used for propagation.

CYLINDRICAL   Cylinder-shaped.

DECUMBENT   Reclining towards the ground, but with an upward-pointed tip.

DEHISCENCE   The opening of ripe fruits to expose seeds.

DICOTYLEDON   *see* cotyledon.

DIMORPHIC   Having two distinct forms.

DIURNAL   Of the day; flowers opening only during the day.

ECHINOCARPUS   Having spiny fruits.

ELLIPSOID   A compressed oval shape (a solid of which all the plane sections through one of the axes are ellipses, and all other sections ellipses or circles).

ENDEMIC   Regular, found in a specified region.

EPIDERMIS   The outer cell layer of a plant.

EPIPHYTE   A plant growing on (but usually not nourished by) another plant.

FAMILY   Botanically, a group of one or more similar genera — usually ends with 'aceae', such as Cactaceae.

FASCIATION   A malformation of plant stem, resulting in a flattened, massed and enlarged crest (found in cristata forms of cacti).

FIELD NUMBER   A number allocated by a collector on collecting plants in their native habitat. Usually preceded by the initials of the collector's name and attached to the recognized name of the plant's genus and species. Useful marker for plants without properly registered names or those that have been re-collected by several authors in different locations at different times.

FILAMENT   The stalk that supports the pollen sac (anther).

FUNNELFORM   A flower shape created by an upwardly widening flower tube.

GENUS   Botanically, a subdivision of a family, consisting of one or more species that show similar characteristics and appear to have a common ancestry. Plural 'genera'.

GLABROUS   Smooth-skinned, without hair or spines.

GLOBOSE   Shaped like a globe; spherical, or nearly so.

GLOCHID   A barbed hair or bristle (as in *Opuntia*).

HABITAT   The natural home or environment of a plant or animal.

HOLOTYPE   The original type specimen used in defining a species.

HYBRID   The offspring of a cross between plants of unlike genetic constitution.

IMPERFECT   Applied to flowers in which any normal part is wanting — a flower that lacks either stamens or pistils (male or female parts respectively).

LACERATE   Having deep and irregular cuts along the edges or point.

LACTEUS   Of the nature of milk, refers to sap which resembles milk, as in *Mammillaria*.

LANATE   Having a long, soft, woolly covering, as in *Epostoa*.

LANCEOLATE   Like a spear-head in shape, tapering.

LINEATE   Marked with stripes or lines.

LOBIVOID   Used to describe a flower shape of typical *Lobivia* type, that is, a wide-opening, funnelform flower.

MAMILLA   Nipple-shaped organ or protuberance; a tubercle, for instance.

MONOECIOUS   Having separate male and female flowers on the same plant.

MONSTROSE   Described as forma monstrosa(-us) — a rare, genetic defect in plants which causes elongation from all growing points (areoles) in an anomalous fashion. See also cristate and fasciated growth forms.

MORPHOLOGY   The science of form; botanically, the structure and form of plants.

MUTABILIS   Not consistent, changeable.

MUTATION   A sudden variation in the hereditary material of a cell.

MUTANT   A plant that has acquired a heritable variation as a result of mutation.

NAPIFORM   A thickened body or root form of growth resembling a carrot-like shape with or without restriction at the point where the roots join onto the plant's body.

NOCTURNAL   Flowers that open at night only.

OBLIQUE   Having sides that are unequal or asymmetrical.

OBOVOID or OVATE   Egg-shaped, with narrower end forming the base.

OFFSET   A side shoot, or lateral branch, which has a growing tip and can produce a new plant.

OVARY   The reproductive organ in which seeds (ovules) are formed after pollination.

OVULE   The part of the ovary of a plant containing the egg cell, which, after fertilisation, develops into a seed.

PECTINATE   To fit together in alternation like the teeth of a comb; shaped like a comb with parallel spines.

PERENNIAL   A plant that continues growth from year to year.

PERIANTH   The outermost, non-sexual part of a flower that encloses the stamens and pistils, usually comprising the calyx and corolla.

PERSISTENT   Remaining attached.

PETAL   Modified leaf of the corolla, usually the coloured part of a flower.

PHOTOSYNTHESIS   The process by which green plants synthesise carbohydrates from water and carbon dioxide, using energy from sunlight which is absorbed by chlorophyll in the green tissues.

PILOSE   With a covering of slender, soft hair.

PISTIL   The female (seed-bearing) part of a flower, consisting of the ovary, style and stigma.

PLANT CELL   The basic structural unit of all plants.

PLUMOSE   Feather-like, as in the spines of *M. plumosa*.

PORRECT   Extended horizontally.

PROSTRATE   Growing along the ground.

PRUINOSE   Frosted, covered with wax-like bloom.

RADIANS   Radiating spines, extending in a circle from the areoles.

RECURVED   Spines bent fully backwards.

RIB   The primary vein of a leaf; in a cactus, the parallel ridges or rows of tubercles that form the body.

ROOTSTOCK   Plant material with good rooting properties onto which material with desirable vegetative features is grafted.

ROTATE   Botanically, wheel-shaped, especially of a corolla that is a single petal with a short tube and spreading limb.

SCALE   A modified leaf on the ovary, flower tube or bud of a cactus. A flattened membranous, more-or-less circular plate of cellular tissue, usually a rudimentary or degenerate leaf.

SEPTUM   A dividing wall or partition.

SPECIES   A group of closely related plants, bearing similar characteristics, that intercross freely. A subdivision of a genus. The species name is the second part of the plant's botanical name.

SPINE   A pointed, rigid or bristle-like part of the cactus, a modified leaf.

STAMEN   The pollen-bearing (male) part of the flower, comprising anther and filament.

STIGMA   The portion of the pistil (female part of the flower) that receives the pollen.

STOMA   A small breathing pore on the leaf or stem of plants. Plural 'stomata'.

STYLE   The stalk-like portion of the pistil, connecting the stigma with the ovary.

SUCCULENT   Any plant that has water storage tissue in the leaf, root or stem.

SYMMETRICAL   A shape that can be divided into two identical halves.

SYNONYM   A new name given to a plant incorrectly, as it had been previously validly named.

SYSTEMIC DISEASE   A disease in which a single infection results in a spread of the disease throughout the whole plant.

SYSTEMIC FUNGICIDE   A fungicide that is absorbed by the plant and moves in the sap to all parts of the plant.

TERETE   Used to describe a cylindrical shape of slightly tapering form of a cactus body, seed-pod or ovary. *Sub-terete* means a cylindrical shape that tapers downward.

TOMENTOSE   Covered with down or dense, woolly hair.

TUBE   A hollow cylindrical channel, the united basal portion of the flower.

TUBERCLE   A conical protuberance which carries an areole, as in *Mammillaria* or *Coryphantha*.

TRUNCATE   Ending abruptly as if cut off at the tip, as in the leaf of *Zygocactus truncatus*.

TYPE LOCALITY   The place from which the type specimen was collected.

VARIETY   A group of plants within a species or subspecies which share similar characteristics, but which differ in respect of those characteristics from other groups within the species. Also used to indicate an improved variant of a cultivated plant — a cultivar.

VASCULAR BUNDLE   Tissue in the centre of the plant stem consisting of a cluster of strands that conduct water and minerals from the roots to the plant.

XEROPHYTE   Plants, such as cacti and succulents, that are adapted to survive on a limited supply of water.

ZYGOMORPHIC   Symmetrical about a single plane, divisible into similar lateral halves in only one way, as in *Zygocactus*.

BIBLIOGRAPHY AND FURTHER READING

Backeberg, C. (1966), *Kakteenlexicon* (in German), VEB Gustav Fisher Verlag, Jena, West Germany.

Backeberg, C. (1976), *Cactus Lexicon* (edited by W. Haage), translated into English by L. Glass, Blandford Press Ltd, Dorset.

Benson, L. (1977), *The Cacti of Arizona*, 3rd edn, University of Arizona Press, Tucson, Arizona.

Benson, Lyman (1982), *The Cacti of the United States and Canada*, Stanford University Press, Stanford, California.

Britton N. L. & Rose J. N. (1921), *The Cactaceae*, 2 volumes, Dover Publishing Co., New York.

Brinkmann, K. (1976), *Sulcorebutia* (in German), Deutsche Kakteen Gesellschaft, Stenhart KG, 7820 Titisee, Neustadt, West Germany.

Buxbaum, F. (1958), *Cactus Culture*, translated into English by V. Higgins, Blandford Press Ltd, Dorset.

Cronquist, A. (1984), *An Integrated System of Classification of Flowering Plants*, Columbia University Press, New York.

Cullmann, W., Goetz, E. & Groener, G., (1984), *Kakteen* (in German), Verlag E. Ulmer Co., Wollgrasweg 41, 7000 Stuttgart 70, Hohenheim, West Germany.

Hecht, H. (1982), *BLV Handbuch der Kakteen* (in German), BLV Verlagsgesellschaft mbH, München, West Germany.

Pilbeam, John (1987), *Cacti for the Connoisseur*, Timber Press, Portland, Oregon.

Rausch, W. (1975), *Lobivia, the Day-Flowering Echinopsidinae*, translated into English by J. Donald, R. Herzig, A-1040 Wienn, Johann Straussgasse 30, Austria.

Ritter, F. (1972), *Kakteen in Südamerika* (in German), 4 volumes, Steinhart KG, 7820 Titisee, Neustadt, West Germany.

Taylor-Marhall, W. & Woods, R. S. (1945), *Glossary of Succulent Plant Terms*, Abbey Garden Press, Pasadena, California.

Weniger, D. (1984), *Cacti of Texas and Neighbouring States, Field Guide*, University of Texas Press, Austin, Texas.

INDEX